PRINCIPLES OF
MICROECONOMICS

BRUCE McCLUNG

third edition

Kendall Hunt
publishing company

Kendall Hunt
publishing company
www.kendallhunt.com
Send all inquiries to:
4050 Westmark Drive
Dubuque, IA 52004-1840

Text + website ISBN 978-1-5249-6893-9
Text ISBN 978-1-5249-6894-6

Published in the United States of America

TABLE OF CONTENTS

Chapters:

1. What Can Microeconomics Do For You? 1

2. Why Do People Trade? 9

3. How Do Markets Work? 23

4. How Much Less Do I Buy When the Price Rises? 45

5. How Do People Decide What to Buy? 61

6. How Are Outputs and Costs Generated? 63

7. What Does (Perfect) Competition Mean?. 75

8. What Does Monopoly Mean?. 91

9. Monopolistic Competition and Oligopoly 99

CHAPTER ONE:

What Can Microeconomics Do For You?

Before you can know what Microeconomics can do for you, you have to know what it is and what it is not; the distinction between Macroeconomics and Microeconomics needs to be made. *Macroeconomics* studies the economy at the national level. Concepts and definitions include: Gross Domestic Product (GDP), the total value of an economy's production; the rate of inflation, or simply inflation, the trends of an index of prices in an economy; and the unemployment rate, how many workers have no job. Macroeconomics topics are frequently discussed in the media e.g., much attention is focused on the first Friday of each month when the Bureau of Labor Statistics releases the previous month's unemployment rate. As a result, when the general public thinks about what economics means, they think about macroeconomics. As we shall see, *Microeconomics* deals with how individual decision makers make choices.

What can my profession, economics, do for you? Specifically, what can microeconomics do for you? The usual course descriptions don't provide much insight or inspiration. At Texas State University, the description of Principles of Microeconomics reads as follows:

> *"An introduction to the microeconomics of a modern industrial society. Emphasis is on supply and demand, cost and price concepts, market structures, income distribution, and similar issues."*

This offers little information or intellectual arousal. Unsurprisingly, the first day of class is devoid of excitement or anticipation, replaced with, instead, dread and apprehension and an expectation of boredom. An unfortunate situation because microeconomics can be both useful and interesting. Of course, microeconomics can never provide as much inherent interest and stimulation as, say, a class on human sexuality.

What can you expect from microeconomics, first intellectually and second pragmatically? Microeconomics improves decision making and enhances understanding of business and social issues. But "How?" By building simple yet revealing models of human behavior that impart a more informed and precise way of thinking. Some of the behavior examined will be personal: for example, the decision to go to college. Other issues will be business oriented: how do firms profit maximize, to name one. Still other topics will be social and, therefore, political in nature: ways to lessen our collective carbon footprint.

Before constructing our first model of behavior, it proves useful to examine the ins and outs of model building. Models characterize all formal intellectual thinking. Astrophysicists, philosophers, musicians all make use of models. Why? For every discipline and everyone in those disciplines, holding the totality of the world in one's consciousness proves impossible. Human limitations require abstraction of the world into a simplification: a model. A well-constructed model captures the variables most relevant to the behavior in question. Just as importantly, one wants to discover variables irrelevant to the behavior in the same question. Frequently the modeling process will require starting from uncomplicated beginnings, ignoring variables that will be included later. The other desirable result of developing a model is the ability to make predictions. Using empirical techniques, the predictions of the model can be tested to see if the model bears and relevance to the behavior in the same question.

There are, of course, misunderstanding about model building. That people must actually and literally behave as the model supposes is a common misunderstanding. It is impossible to know if a description of any sort of behavior is the **actual** way the world acts. The assessment of the accuracy a given model results from looking at its prognostications and disproving them or not[1]. If anyone—researcher, professor, politician, or advocate—says he knows how people behave based on his or someone else's model, they are either ignorant or manipulative.

The first and most elemental economic model is a statement of what people are trying to achieve. A **Rational, Optimizing Individual (ROI)** is an individual who faces resource limitations and possesses preferences, makes choices to optimize his economic well-being.[2] The contention here is **everyone** acts to maximize this economic well-being: you, Bill Gates, the homeless, firms, governments, everyone.

Do people *really* behave in the ROI way? Maybe; one can only assert that people behave as if to optimize their economic well-being, a seeming reasonable supposition. By explicitly modeling the most basic behavior of individuals, one can build more complex models to examine and possibly explain more complex behavior. It also becomes easier to notice mistakes made in reasoning. Finally, insight can be gleaned from situations in which the economic theory predicts behavior should be this but people behave like that.

Development of some basic concept comes next. Many of these ideas you have observed already but not in a formal context. Please note the following concepts are **not** hypothesized models. Rather, they are statements of reality which form the rational, optimizing individual's environment.

Basic Concepts and Definitions

The pervasive element of the environment all rational, optimizing individuals exist in is *scarcity*: possessing unlimited wants, all individuals—consumers, firms, and governments—have only limited resources available to fulfill their wants. It is best to break up the definition of scarcity into two parts and examine them independently.

---

[1] In formal statistical hypothesis testing, one never confirms the "truth" of a model. One either disproves its claims or fails to disprove. Failing to disprove a model's prediction is far different than confirming a model's prediction. The best statement a model builder gets is "we cannot show the model is an incorrect description of behavior."

[2] Are other postulates of behavior possible? Most certainly. Will they be discussed as to compare the relative accuracy or morality of these alternatives to the ROI model? No, because there are other forums designed for just such debates elsewhere.

The first part, that individuals have unlimited wants, requires a thought experiment. Suppose one were asked to make a list of the 10 most important goods (iPhone, pizza, etc.) or services (a wedding ceremony, cellar carrier, etc.) one wants to have. That's fairly easy to do. Next comes a request to expand the list to 100 items. It certainly takes longer to do, but doesn't prove impossible. Finally, one is asked to enlarge the list to 1,000 items. A very tedious task to be sure but it could be done. The result of the thought experiment is, apparently, wants are unlimited.[3]

Second, the limitations of resources are self-evident. The constraint which all of us, from the poorest person to the richest government, must contend is the limitation of time. Only 24 hours exist in a day. No one can add to or subtract from the 1,440 minutes which defines a day. The limitations of our natural resources are well discussed today. The last barrel of oil must exist somewhere in the ground. Likewise, only so many people are available to work (not the number that are working, but the number that could be working). The number of machines used in the manufacture of iPhones is finite. What about solar energy? At night sunshine seems to be in short supply and in 4.7 billion years the sun will fade away. Only so many cubic feet of air surround our planet; although the number may seem infinite it is not. All of the world's resources are fixed even if conceiving the immensity of some of the limitations proves impossible.

The existence of scarcity produces a very important implication: all ROIs (Rational, Optimizing Individuals) must make choices. Unlike resources, choices are unlimited. Everyone picks from an infinite number of alternatives. Where do we live?; what kind and how much education do we complete?; where do we work?; do we get married? and so forth. Then, having made a choice-say, get married,—there are endless subsequent choices: do we get divorced?; do we have children?; etcetera. The total possible sequences of choices defies comprehension. Everyone reading this chapter could try out for a TV talent show to become the next famous pop singer. Few, however, will ever make the choice to try out because they, like the author, possess no musical talent.

The concept of cost follows directly from making a choice: because to choose one thing, all other choices are given up. It is the giving up that generates the concept of cost. Suppose you have one hour that remains unplanned. You imagine a list of the activities you could pursue and notice the list is infinitely long but you also recognize time is the fixed resource. You have ranked the activities from most important to least important. The list shows studying for your exam in English literature as the number one, most valuable activity and so you choose to spend your hour studying. No dollars are being exchanged in this choice so the measurement of cost must be in some other form. Return to the list of ranked activities. Note which choice came in second place, the next most valuable activity. Suppose it was playing Angry Birds. The hour you spent studying tonight cannot be reclaimed; over your finite lifetime, you will have spent one less hour playing Angry Birds than was possible. The value you place on an hour's worth of Angry Birds playing forms the cost of your choice to study. The **opportunity cost** of a choice is the next most valuable choice not selected.

---

[3] In this day of viridity and carbon footprints, one might be tempted to debate the merits of unlimited wants, i.e., should people have unlimited wants? Do not debate; simply accept, for the duration of this class, unlimited wants is the reality.

Before examining how rational, optimizing individuals make decisions, a word about preferences. To be clear, it is not assumed all ROIs will reach the same outcome for a given set of circumstances. Everyone develops a unique set of preferences. Some like Coke, others Pepsi. Neither choice is correct. This is how two people can be given exactly the same set of conditions but make significantly different choices, leading to very dissimilar outcomes. More will be said about preferences when other models of analysis are added later.

To recap, unlimited wants with limited resources leads inexorably to choices. Making a choice immediately excludes all other choices, generating an opportunity cost. How, then, do rational, optimizing individuals make optimal choices? What model of decision making leads to the most desirable choices? How do ROI's ensure they are not selecting the third or fourth most important choice from the list of activities rather than the first? At least three possibilities present themselves. First, rational, optimizing individuals can make choices randomly. Second, ROI's can make choices based solely on past behavior. Third is the use of cost/benefit analysis.

Picking petals off a daisy, flipping a coin, throwing darts are all examples of a randomness. One flips a coin and takes the activity assigned to heads or the one associated with tails. Once one decides to let the flip of a coin make the choice, one has no further say. Very few, if any, ROI's would use randomness to make an important decision e.g., whether to get a university education, what university to attend and so forth. A poor choice, something other than the first most important activity, is equally likely using a decision rule of random choice. Suppose the flip of the coin comes up tails, "don't go to university." After the flip, there is no more analysis. The choice is set, end of story. This does not make for an attractive decision rule for a ROI to use.

A second possible decision rule for making choices would be to mimic past behavior. Textbook authors rarely speak from their personal experience; here is an exception. I use Heinz ketchup exclusively. I did not choose Heinz ketchup because I conducted a double blind test, the results of which showed Heinz tasted best. Rather, my Mother always bought Heinz and I just continued to make the same decision into adulthood. The magnitude of the decision is small so use of past behavior will produce an acceptable outcome; however, there may be a ketchup which better suits my preferences that I will never know about. When it comes to the important decisions, past behavior certainly plays a role. If both parents got university educations then there is a significant likelihood their children will obtain a university education. Which university one attends can be strongly influenced by past behavior. At Texas A&M University, there is a noticeable tendency for the children of A&M graduates to attend A&M as well. The relationship between past behavior and current behavior, particularly across generations, can be statistically strong. The limitation of modeling behavioral choices this way is obvious: someone had to make the initial choice in order for something to be mimicked. Assuming the first university educated generation in a family did not make the decision randomly, what model did they use? A decision rule for rational, optimizing individuals which likely produces the optimal choice remains elusive.

What decision rule goes beyond simple random choice or past behavior? What decision rule produces the optimal choices for a rational, optimizing individual? What decision rule takes both the chooser's preferences into account and compares alternatives? Its name is the **Cost/Benefit Rule**: individuals should pursue an activity as long as the extra benefits from the activity exceed the extra cost of the activity, stopping when the two are equal. Unlike the two previous rules, the Cost/Benefit Rule allows the chooser to determine the benefits and costs of various alternatives. The Cost/Benefit Rule results from efforts to maximize Total Economic Surplus (TES).

Total Economic Surplus (TES) is the difference between the Total Benefits (TB) and the Total Costs (TC) of an activity, TES = TB − TC. Economics presumes total economic surplus maximization forms the primary goal of rational, optimizing individuals.[4] Some would doubtless argue other goals are more important, or that many of the social problems today stem directly from individuals maximizing total economic surplus. This issue will not be examined here.

Before exploring a specific application of TES, a few qualifications are in order. Recalling the misunderstanding that for a model to be legitimate, ROIs must follow it explicitly. The model's validity is not based on ROI's taking out pencil and paper and making numerical calculation of TES. Economists argue, instead, that people behave **as if** they make these calculations at some intuitive level. TES is the best approximation for economic behavior of ROI's developed so far. In some cases, explicit calculations may, in fact, occur. Choosing which university to attend could lead to calculations of the lowest tuition/scholarship combination weighted against the quality of the school, assessed by the ranking in US News & World Reports. Deciding where to live will pit the desirability of location against the purchasing power of the salary/regional cost-of-living combination. When a rational, optimizing individual decides to go to the movies, he does not give a lot of explicit thought to a weighing of the costs and benefits. That does not mean on an intuitive plane he is not considering benefits and costs.

Second, it is sometimes necessary to view the values of the benefits and costs of activities conceptually, i.e., the values are nonmarket transactions. The benefits and/or costs of activities can, and must, be made monetary even if they are not normally thought of as being monetary. For example, the enjoyment (benefit) of playing Angry Birds for an hour is not expressed as a dollar amount. Playing the game is simply enjoyable. But conceptually, the playing of Angry Birds for an hour can be thought of as having a monetary value. Maybe playing for an hour is worth, say, $50. Conceptualizing the monetary value of the benefit of a nonmarket activity does not require it has be the same for everyone. For someone else, who is not much of a fan of playing games, the value of Angry Bird playing might be considerably less.

Similarly, negative events without explicit dollar values can also be treated conceptually. The cost of driving from point A to point B is comprised of two parts: one naturally monetary, one not. Expenditures for gas plus wear and tear on the car are explicit monetary costs and can be easily measured. The frustration of sitting in traffic is obviously a cost of getting from A to B but does not have an explicit monetary value. To correctly apply the TES model, all costs must be counted. The notion that all actions, market based or nonmarket based, can be described by a

---

[4] The mathematically inclined student can observe this is an application of the first order condition of a maximization problem. Formally, if TES = TB(activity) − TC(activity), then to maximize TES, set TB'(activity) = TC'(activity) where TB' and TC' are the first derivatives of TB and TC respectively.

monetary value permeates economics. To succeed in understanding economics, one must be able to accept that nonmarket activities can be made in to monetary values, If this sounds perfectly reasonable to you, you might consider changing your major to economics.

Consider a formal example of the Total Economic Surplus model. Suppose you are deciding what to do on Saturday. Out of the infinite number of possibilities, you narrow the list to three alternatives: working, hiking in the wildlife refuge, or watching a Law and Order marathon on TNT. Going to work is your usual activity on Saturday, earning you $100, which is the total benefit. The cost of commuting to work is ignored for convenience. Not going to work requires you take an unpaid sick day. Going hiking has a value to you of $70 (conceptual dollar value) along with a $30 entrance fee (explicit dollar value). Watching the Law and Order marathon has a value to you of $35 dollars (conceptual dollar value) and has no monetary fee. The cable bill is not counted as a cost because you pay your cable bill regardless of whether you watch the marathon or not: this is not a pay-per-view event.

One attempt to calculate the TES for the hiking adventure might be $70 − $30 = $40. This is but a naive calculation. To account for all the costs properly, the opportunity cost of taking the unpaid day off from work must be included. The $100 you could have earned is gone; you cannot make it up. Therefore, the accurate calculation of the TES of hiking is $70 − $30 − $100 = −$60. Similarly, the correct calculation of the TES for watching Law & Order is $35 − 0 − $100 = −$65. Both alternatives to working produce negative TES values. No one will ever select an activity with a negative TES. Sadly then, you will be going to work because the TES of work is positive: $60 (= $100 − $0 − ($70−$30)). The ($70−$30) term in the calculation is the net benefit of hiking; it must be included as a cost because the value of the next best alternative must *always* be counted.

Many of you have faced a similar circumstance (maybe not hiking specifically but some activity you enjoy) and decided to go hiking anyway. Does this fact render the economic model of a rational, optimizing individual applying the cost/benefit useless? Not at all. You control the conceptual value of the benefits to going hiking or watching Law & Order. If you are dying to go hiking, you might reevaluate the benefit to be $200. Now the TES is $200 − $30 − $100 = $70, so you go hiking and see wildlife.

You now have an idea of what microeconomic can do for you. But why should you care? Throughout your life you are going to make many important decisions. Some decisions you will make based on intuition; others may require a somewhat more explicit use of the tools being developed here. Studying economic models helps in making better choices as you seek to maximize Total Economic Surplus.

The next section introduces several additional behavioral models common in economics. The following discussions are not meant to be comprehensive; it is merely a preview. The models will receive greater attention in future chapters. For example, game theory will be the major focus of Chapter Nine, Why Do People Confess?

Tools of Analysis

So far, our analytical toolkit contains two models: the Rational, Optimizing Man and the Cost/Benefit Rule. With these two tools (the terms model and tool are interchangeable), one can conduct a substantial amount of analysis. With the limited number of models, important conclusion were still reached, e.g., failure to factor in opportunity costs results in less than optimal choices. With the more intricate models discussed next, analysis of economic behavior extends significantly.

Marginal Analysis

Recall the definition of a rational, optimizing individual: when faced with choices and given our preferences, one acts in such a way as to optimize his economic well-being. Frequently, a ROI , in an effort to properly apply the Cost/Benefit Rule, must make comparisons of small changes in the benefits and costs of an activity. *Marginal Analysis*, then refers to using small (marginal) changes to make choices. Take the following example:

TABLE 1					
	Hours Spent Studying Economics				
	0	**1**	**2**	**3**	**4**
Score on Economics Test	40	65	80	90	95
Score on Physics Test	60	55	45	30	0

You have decided to spend a total of 4 hours studying for 2 upcoming exams: one in economics, the other in physics. You can spend all 4 hours on one of them, all 4 hours on the other or spend time on both. As a ROI, you want to make an optimal decision. First, note the limited resource is time; you have decided to allot a total of 4 hours. The choice is how to allocate the 4 hours between economics and physics. Secondly, your preferences are to do as well in physics as economics. That is, a one point improvement in your economics test score is as valuable to you as a one point improvement in your physics test score. If you were, say, an economics major, you might have different preferences. A one point improvement in your physics test score might be less valuable than a one point improvement in your economics test score.

To locate the optimal solution, one must calculate the **marginal benefit (MB)**, the additional benefit of an activity derived from a small increase in the activity, and the **marginal cost (MC)**, the additional cost of an activity from a small increase in the activity. The marginal benefit is the increase in the economics test score from another hour of studying economics and the marginal cost is the reduction in the physics test score from studying physics for one less hour. Thus the MB of the first hour spent studying economics is a 25 point (65 − 40) improvement in your test score; the marginal cost is a 5 point (60 − 55) reduction in your physics exam score. The MB of the second hour studying economics is 15 (80 − 65) and the MC is 10 (55 − 45). The MB of the third hour is 10 (90 − 80) while its marginal cost is 15 (45 − 30). The fourth hour's marginal benefit is 5 (95 − 90) with a MC of 30 (30 − 0). The Cost/Benefit Rule states activities should be continued as long as the marginal benefit is greater than or equal to the marginal cost. The first hour of studying economics is worthwhile (MB = 25 > 5 = MC); the second hour of studying economics is also justified (MB = 15 > 10 = MC).

The third hour of economics studying is not a wise choice (MB = 10 < 15 = MC). While your score in economics does improve from an 80 to a 90 when you study economics for three hours, it comes at a cost of a 15 point reduction in your physics test score; a poor tradeoff. It is useful to note the benefit of the fourth hour of economics studying is 5 while the cost is 30, an even worse tradeoff. In any MB, MC exercise, once you have located the point where the activity's MB is less than the activity's MC, it never switches back. In other words, the MB of the fourth hour would never jump back up to, say 13, and the MC of the fourth hour does not drop back down to, say 9. By using the tool of marginal analysis, you should spend 2 hours studying economics and 2 hours studying physics. The wisdom of the splitting the 4 hours into 2 for economics and 2 for physics is confirmed by summing the test scores, which results in 125 points. No other allocation produces a greater value.

Consider a practical and relevant application. Suppose you are close to making A's or B's in three of the classes you are taking this semester. Just a little more effort studying and you will do well enough on the final exams to achieve the A's and B's. In the fourth class you are enrolled in, economics, you have a solid C. Many students in this situation adopt a strategy of studying economics a lot, attempting to get a B. An optimal solution is unlikely to result from this approach. A better solution would be to spend your limited study time on the three other classes to ensure you get your A's and B's and only study economics as much as you have been and take your C. If you allocate most of your studying time to economics, you will have less time to prepare for those three other classes and those grades go from A's and B's to B's and C's. And you will probably end up with a C in economics anyway.

The end of our introduction to microeconomics is reached. The rest of the book is devoted to expanding the range and depth of economic models in the toolkit. Chapters 2, 3, and 4 establish the basics of microeconomics. Chapter 5 examines in greater detail the factors influencing the behavior of buyers. Chapters 6, 7 and 8 study the conduct of different types of businesses. The next chapter, "Why Do People Interact?" gets the ball of understanding rolling. I humbly hope I have pique your interest in the microeconomics and demonstrated some of its usefulness.

CHAPTER TWO:

Why Do People Trade?

The first chapter presented the basic concepts of economics. With them, a good deal of the observed world can be understood. The basic concepts, however, shed no light on why a rational, optimizing individual would interact, at least economically, with another rational, optimizing individual. Obviously, this needs explanation because economic interactions characterize a great deal of our daily activities. Going to work; buying a 6 shot espresso; watching the evening news are all examples of economic trades. Chapter Two, then, provides an answer to the essential question "Why do people trade?"

NOTES

Absolute and Comparative Advantage

For rational, optimizing individuals to want to interact economically, they both must have something to offer one another. Otherwise, trade is unlikely. The example to be presented is an "island economy," where there are only two economic activities—two tasks—and only two people performing them. This approach seems contrived and it is, but by starting with a less complex model, the major points will be clearer. The two people on our island are Ryan and Chase. The two tasks are washing loads of dishes ("LOADS") and folding shirts ("SHIRTS"). The data is displayed in Table 2.1.

TABLE 2.1		
	Loads of Dishes per Hour	**Shirts Folded per Hour**
Ryan	6	30
Chase	2	20

The first definition is absolute advantage: an individual has an *absolute advantage* over another person is he can produce more output in a given time period than the other person. Looking at Table 2.1, we see that Ryan can wash 6 loads of dishes in one hour while Chase can only wash 2 loads in one hour. Therefore, Ryan possesses an absolute advantage in the washing of dishes. As for the folding of shirts, Ryan again has the absolute advantage. He can fold 30 shirts in one hour while Chase can only fold 20 shirts in an hour. Why Ryan is superior in the production of washed dishes and folded shirts is unknown and unexplained.[1] It is simply given that Ryan performs better at both tasks.

---

[1] Speculation as to why this is true is unnecessary and unprofitable.

Measuring absolute advantage by output per period (loads of dishes per hour and folded shirts per hour) is only one way to frame the discussion. One could change the specification of Table 2.1 to time per unit of output. The columns in Table 2.1 would read "Time to Wash One Load of Dishes" and "Time to Fold One Shirt." For Ryan to wash one load of dishes requires 10 minutes (60 minutes divided by 6 loads). Chase needs 30 minutes to wash one load. Chase requires 3 minutes to fold a shirt (60 minutes divided by 20 folded shirts) while Ryan needs 2 minutes to fold a shirt. The data continue to show Ryan possessing an absolute advantage over Chase for both tasks. When working any comparative advantage exercise, one can either hold the amount of time constant and measure how much output is produced or one can hold the amount of output constant and measure how much time it takes to produce the output. Preference will be given to the output per period measurement.

Importantly, absolute advantage does not explain why people trade. The incentive to trade flows from **comparative advantage**. An individual has a comparative advantage over another individual if he has a lower opportunity cost of producing output that the other person. Ryan's possession of an absolute advantage in the production of both washed loads of dishes and folded shirts might strongly tempt one to presume there is no opportunity for Ryan and Chase to interact economically, i.e., Chase has nothing to offer Ryan. Before adopting that conclusion, the comparative advantage measures for Ryan and Chase need to assessed.

To appraise comparative advantage, one first needs to calculate the opportunity costs of production for Ryan and Chase. The calculations for Ryan and Chase are presented in Tables 2.2[2] and 2.3.[3] What is the opportunity cost (how much is given up) when Ryan washes one more load of dishes? The cost is expressed as the number of shirts going unfolded. Look to the first line of the first row in Table 2.2. One wants to know how much is sacrificed when Ryan washes **one** load of dishes. Divide the number of loads washed by 6. Dividing by a 6 "normalizes" the number of loads of washed dishes to a 1. Treating line one as an equation, the same action must be performed on the other cell. Meaning 30 will be divided by 6, resulting in a 5. Thus when Ryan washes one more load of dishes, the opportunity cost is that 5 shirts go unfolded.

TABLE 2.2		
	Loads of Dishes per Hour	**Shirts Folded per Hour**
Ryan	$6/6 = 1$	$30/6 = 5$
	$6/30 = 1/5 = 0.20$	$30/30 = 1$
Chase	2	20

It is also necessary to know how many loads of dishes are not washed because Ryan folds one more shirt. After resetting the values in the table to their original amounts, 6 and 30, repeat the same procedure going from left to right. This is illustrated in

---

[2] In the row for Ryan there are now two lines in each of the cells. In the text, "line one" refers to $6/6 = 1$; $30/6 = 5$. "Line two" refers to $6/30 = 1/5 = 0.20$; $30/30 = 1$.

[3] In the row for Chase there are now two lines in each of the cells. In the text, "line one" refers to $2/2 = 1$; $20/2 = 10$. "Line two" refers to $2/20 = 1/10 = 0.10$; $20/20 = 1$.

line two of the first row in Table 2.2. Divide both sides by 30. The value of folded shirts is now normalized to 1. Ryan's opportunity cost of a folded shirt is 6/30 or 1/5 or 0.20. When Ryan folds one more shirt, 20 percent of a washed load of dishes is lost. The mathematically astute will note that one could take the reciprocal of the opportunity cost of washing one load of dishes to find the opportunity cost of folding a single shirt.

TABLE 2.3		
	Loads of Dishes per Hour	**Shirts Folded per Hour**
Ryan	6	30
Chase	2/2 = 1	20/2 = 10
	2/20 = 1/10 = 0.10	20/20 =1

In order for comparative advantage to be meaningful, identical calculations must be made for Chase. The technique will be same the one used for Ryan and is illustrated in Table 2.3. First, what is the opportunity cost (how many folded shirts are sacrificed) when Chase washes one load of dishes? To normalize the number of washed loads of dishes to a 1, divide line one in the second row by 2. Since line one is an "equation," the value of folded shirts must also be divided by a 2, resulting in 10. When Chase washes one load of dishes, 10 shirts are not folded. Next, the procedure must be reversed. In line two of the second row, the number of folded shirts is divided by 20 to form a ratio equal to 1.To keep balance, the value of loads of washed dishes, 2, is divided by 20. Simplifying the fraction leads to 1/10 or 0.10. When Chase folds one shirt, 10 percent of a load of dishes is unwashed. As before, once one opportunity cost is calculated, the other opportunity cost can be located by taking the reciprocal.

With opportunity costs calculated for both individuals and both tasks, who possesses the comparative advantage in which task can be determined The calculations show that for washing dishes, Ryan's opportunity cost is 5 unfolded shirts while Chase's opportunity cost is 10 unfolded shirts. Clearly, less is given up (fewer shirts go unfolded) when Ryan washes dishes than when Chase washes dishes. Therefore, Ryan has the comparative advantage in washing dishes. On the other hand, Chase's opportunity cost of folding shirts is 0.10; 10 percent of one load of dishes goes unwashed when Chase folds a shirt. When Ryan folds a shirt, 20 percent of a load of dishes go unwashed because Ryan's opportunity cost is 0.20. The calculations in Tables 2.2 and 2.3 show less is given up if Chase folds shirts. He is not more efficient that Ryan in an absolute sense—Table 2.1 reveals he is not. But in a relative sense, Chase is more efficient that Ryan at folding shirts.

The above discussion highlights the cornerstone of why humans trade. The **Rule of Comparative Advantage** proposes that everyone is better off concentrating on those activities for which they have a comparative advantage, i.e., the lowest opportunity costs. In the example above, the society made up of Ryan and Chase is better off if Ryan focuses on washing dishes while Chase focuses on folding shirts. This point will be examined in more detail shortly.

The principle of comparative advantage should be used in one of the critical decision of your life: which subject to major in. How can the rule of comparative advantage be applied to your decision? Suppose your math skills are not good. Not because you have been unwilling to study; rather you simply do not "get" mathematics. Art History, on the other hand, is your passion. You find the topic infinitely interesting. You have been studying it on your own since junior high school. No matter how much civil engineers are being paid and no matter how much external pressure may being exerted on you to become a civil engineer, you and society will suffer if you choose engineering. Society will benefit more if you choose the major for which you find it easy to produce, that is, for which your opportunity costs are the lowest. By choosing civil engineering, where you do not have a comparative advantage, you will produce less than someone who does have a comparative advantage. If you major in Art History, society would see greater output because you would produce relatively more Art History analysis. Society realizes a smaller total output of goods and services if you fail to apply the rule of comparative advantage.

Production Possibilities Curves

So far the discussion has been limited to the maximum number of shirts folded or dishes washed; the end points. Now the analysis will encompass the complete relationship between the number of washed loads of dishes and the number of folded shirts. Using the data from Table 2.1, one can construct graphs of the island economy, shown in Figure 2.1. Loads of dishes (LOADS) are measured on the vertical axis while folded shirts (SHIRTS) are measured on the horizontal axis. On the vertical axis, the increment is 1 unit; each tick mark represents 1 load of washed dishes. The range of values on the vertical goes from 0 to 10. For the horizontal axis, the increment is 5 units; each hash mark represents 5 folded shirts. The range for folded shirts is 0 to 60. The measurements of output are per hour just as in the table. The choice of which activity to place on which axis is entirely arbitrary; the same conclusion would be reached if the axes were reversed.

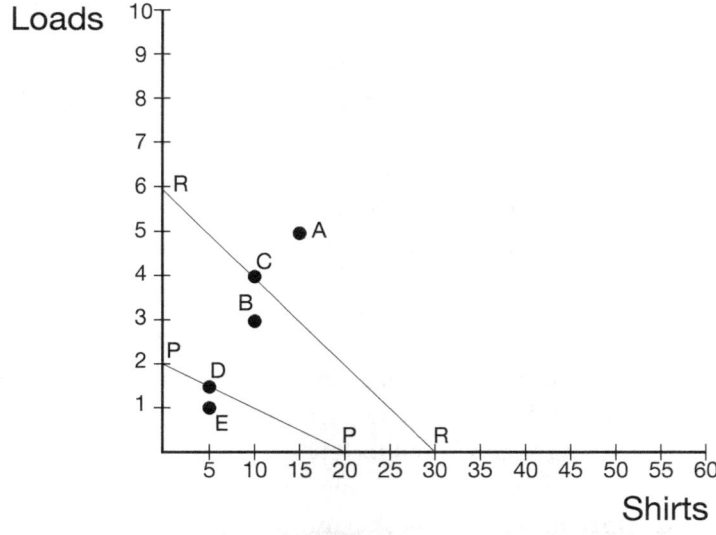

FIGURE 2.1

Returning to Table 2.1, Ryan can wash 6 loads of dishes and fold zero shirts. When describing graphed points, the horizontal axis value is listed first. The point (0,6) in Figure 2.1 then represents Ryan's maximum production of washed dishes. At the other extreme, when Ryan produces zero loads of washed dishes, he folds 30 shirts, making the point to plot (30,0). Recall a linear relationship can be determined from two points. Running a line through (0,6) and (30,0), reveals the various combinations of folded shirts and washed dishes Ryan could produce in the course of an hour. For example, the point (15,3)is one of the points on the line. Over an hour, Ryan could produce 3 loads of washed dishes and 15 folded shirts. Similarly, Chase's data can be transported from the table to the graph. When he folds no shirts, Chase's maximum production of loads of washed dishes per hour is 2: the point to graph is then (0,2). When he produces no washed dishes, Chase can fold 20 shirts. The plotted point is (20,0). After these two points are plotted, a straight line can be extended between them. The line shows, as it did for Ryan, the combinations of washed dishes and folded shirts Chase can produce if he splits his hour between the two. For example, when Chase produces one load of washed dishes, he can fold 10 shirts.

An important model has been constructed in Figure 2.1. A ***production possibilities curve (PPC)*** is a curve[4] illustrating the maximum production of one good or service for each and every level of production of the other good or service. Figure 2.1, therefore, illustrates the production possibilities curves of Ryan and Chase. When Ryan produces zero folded shirts, the maximum output of washed dishes is 6 loads. When 15 shirts are folded, Ryan can, at most, wash 3 loads of dishes. When 30 shirts get folded, the maximum loads of dishes Ryan can wash is zero. The line, labeled **RR**, that passes through the points (0,6) and (30,0) is Ryan's production possibilities curve. For Chase, if he produces zero folded shirts, then the largest number of washed loads of dishes is 2. If he folds 20 shirts, the greatest number of loads of washed dishes is zero. The line, labeled **PP**, connecting the points (0,2) and (20,0) is Chase's production possibilities curve.

The production possibilities curve has several properties. The first and most obvious feature is the negative slope of both Ryan's and Chase's PPC. The slope of any PPC must be negative because a tradeoff is occurring. If Ryan produces more folded shirts, it can only come at the expense of washed dishes. If Chase washes more dishes, he will fold fewer shirts. Scarcity-the fundamental idea of economics-emphasizes limited resources and the requirement for choices to be made. The production possibilities curve illustrates this precisely. First, resources are limited. In each hour, Ryan and Chase have only so much effort to expend on washing dishes or folding shirts or some combination of the two. Second, choices must be made. Both Ryan and Chase must choose how many loads get washed and how many shirts get folded. As they ponder which combination to produce, each must consider the tradeoff between washing dishes and folding shirts. Rather than just guessing, calculation of the numerical value of the slope of the PPC's will quantify the tradeoff.

Earlier, we computed the opportunity cost of an extra folded shirt for both Ryan and Chase. For Ryan, the numerical value was 0.20; one extra folded shirt resulted in a 20% loss of one load of washed dishes. One of the points on his PPC is

---

[4] Figuratively for now.

(10,4.0): 10 folded shirts and 4 loads of washed dishes. If he were to fold one more shirt, we would move down along the PPC and arrive at (11,3.8). The formula for finding the slope of a line with two points is "rise over run" :

$$\Delta LOADS/\Delta SHIRTS,$$

where Δ means change. For Ryan's data, the rise, $\Delta LOADS$, equals $(4 - 3.8)$. The run, $\Delta SHIRTS$, equals $(10 - 11)$. Forming the ratio of rise over run,

$$\Delta LOADS/\Delta SHIRTS = (4 - 3.8)/(10 - 11) = 0.20/-1 = -0.20$$

reveals the slope of Ryan's PPC is -0.20. This is precisely the opportunity cost calculated from the data in Table 2.1

For Chase, the opportunity cost of an extra folded shirt was 10% fewer loads of washed dishes. If Chase folds 10 shirts, he can wash 1 load of dishes or (10,1). Folding one more shirt reduces loads of washed dishes by 10% meaning a movement down Chase's PPC from (10,1) to (11,0.90). Applying the rise over run formula

$$\Delta LOADS/\Delta SHIRTS = (1 - 0.90)/(10 - 11) = 0.10/-1 = -0.10$$

results in the slope of Chase's PPC.[5] In absolute value, the slope of Chase's PPC ($|-0.10| = 0.10$) is smaller than the slope of Ryan's PPC ($|-0.20| = 0.20$), confirming our conclusion that the comparative advantage for folding shirts belongs to Chase. In general, the smaller the absolute value of the slope of a production possibilities curve (the flatter the PPC), the smaller the opportunity cost. The severity of the tradeoff between the two goods is modest. The larger the absolute value (the steeper the PPC), the greater the opportunity cost or the greater the size of the tradeoff between the two goods.

The next property of any production possibilities curve is it divides the area of the graph into available combinations and unavailable combinations. Construction of Ryan's production possibilities curve forms a triangle which defines the area of available combinations. It starts at 0, goes up the LOADS axis to 6, then proceeds down along the PPC to 30 folded shirts and then left along the SHIRTS axis back to zero. Ryan is able to produce any of the infinite points in the area of the triangle. For Chase, the area of his PPC is located by starting at 0, going up to 2 loads of washed dishes and then down and to the left along the line to 20 folded shirts and then back to zero. Chase, like Ryan, can produce any combination of loads of washed dishes and folded shirts in the area of his PPC. Importantly, both Ryan and Chase can produce the combinations on the downward sloping line that defines their respective PPC's.

Having defined the area in which Ryan and Chase can produce, we can also locate the combinations of washed dishes and folded shirts they cannot produce. The area outside of their respective PPC's defines the unavailable combinations. Looking at Ryan's PPC, the combination (15,5), point **A** in Figure 2.1, is outside the triangle and thus unavailable. Ryan can never wash 5 loads of dishes *and* fold 15 shirts. He can wash 5 loads of dishes but will then only have time left to fold 5 shirts. Alternatively, Ryan can fold 15 shirts but will only be able to wash 3 loads of dishes. Ryan can have

---

[5] Formally, the equation of the PPC for Ryan is LOADS = 6 – 0.20 × SHIRTS; the equation for Chase is LOADS = 2 – 0.10 × SHIRTS.

5 loads of washed dishes or 15 folded shirts but he cannot have both. For Chase, point **B**, (10,3) is unavailable. He cannot wash 3 loads of dishes and fold 10 shirts. He can never wash 3 loads of dishes; if he folds 10 shirts, he can wash only a single load of dishes.

Another property of the PPC is it distinguishes points of production that are efficient from those which are inefficient. For Chase, point **D**, (5,1.5), is **efficient**: all available resources are fully utilized. Chase is expending all of his effort in washing loads of dishes and folding shirts, resulting in 1.5 loads of washed dishes and 5 folded shirts. He cannot do more. For Ryan, the combination (10, 4), represented by point **C** in Figure 2.1 is an efficient point; he is expending all of his effort at that point. Any point that lies along the PPC is an efficient point. Alternatively, points that lie inside the production possibilities curve are **inefficient**: all available resources are not engaged. For Chase, point **E** is an inefficient level of production. The production level of (5,1) represents Chase **not** expending all of his effort on producing washed loads of dishes or folded shirts. The combination (10,3), point **B**, is an inefficient level of output for Ryan; he is not using all of his available effort to fold shirts and wash dishes.[6]

The differentiations among the various points in Figure 2.1 may be jumbled. To review, the first distinction is between available points and unavailable points. Available points exist along the production possibilities curve and any point inside the PPC. Any point beyond the PPC can't be produced with the available resources and thus unavailable. From the set of available points, a further classification is made. If a production combination lies along the PPC, then the combination is efficient. If the point is inside the triangle formed by the PPC, the point is inefficient. If the point is unavailable, it is neither efficient nor inefficient; it is simply unavailable.

Social Production Possibilities Curve and Trade

Why will Chase and Ryan engage in trade? Because both will be better off. If Ryan relies exclusively on his ability to produce, he can have 6 loads of washed dishes and 30 folded shirts. If Chase is entirely self-reliant, he can have 2 loads of washed dished or 20 folded shirts. If Ryan and Chase were to interact, they can enjoy greater output. Specifically, 8 loads of washed dishes (6 + 2) or 50 folded shirts (30 + 20). Clearly, Chase benefits to a greater extent than Ryan since Ryan possesses an absolute advantage in the production of both items. Chase's potential number of loads of washed dishes jumps from 2 to 8. The possible number of folded shirts Chase can have grows from 20 to 50. In both cases, Chase has access to substantially more production. Ryan sees smaller increases in his access to production, but critically he **does** see an increase. With respect to loads of washed dishes, he can enjoy 8 loads rather than 6. For folded shirts, the total rises from 30 to 50.

Figure 2.2 illustrates the production possibilities curve for the society made up of Ryan and Chase. The endpoints are 8 loads of washed dishes and 50 folded shirts. Unlike the individual PPC's, one cannot simply run a line through (0,8) and (50,0). Instead, the social production possibilities curve contains a kink. Suppose Ryan

---

[6] Observe that while point **B** is an inefficient combination for Ryan, it is an unavailable point for Chase.

and Chase have decided to interact and have chosen the leftmost endpoint: 8 loads of washed dishes and zero folded shirts. This means they are both spending the entirety of the hour washing loads of dishes. Ryan and Chase now decide they desire some folded shirts. One of them will have to start folding shirts. The question is which rational, optimizing individual should begin folding shirts? Have established earlier Chase's comparative advantage in the folding of shirts, he should be the one to start. The social PPC will mimic Chase's PPC. If you compare the portion of the social PPC from (0,8) to (20,6), it is identical to Chase's PPC.

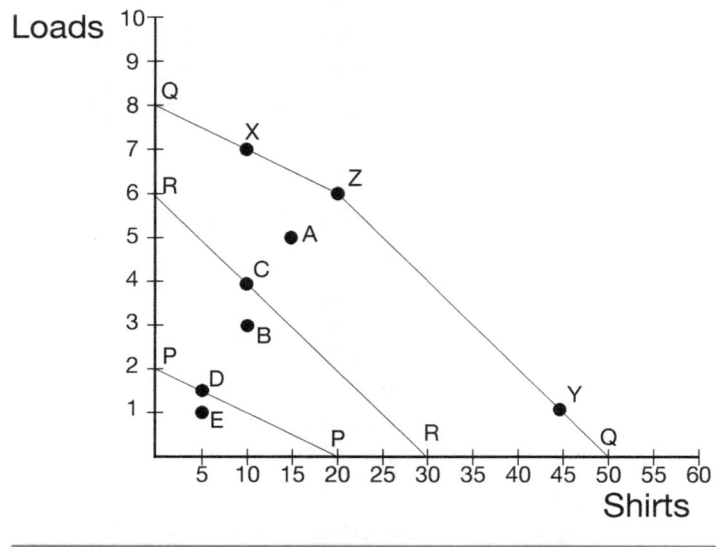

FIGURE 2.2

The social production possibilities curve is always the combination of the efforts of Ryan and Chase. Consider combination (10,7), represented by point *X* in Figure 2.2. To produce this combination, Ryan is spending all his time washing dishes and producing 6 loads. Chase is splitting his time between the two, producing one load of dishes wash and folding 10 shirts. The point on the social PPC is composed of the combined production of Chase and Ryan. The point (10,7) is a summary of the point (10+0,1+6), where 10+0 is the decomposed production of folded shirts and 1+6 is the decomposed production of loads of washed dishes. Writing the point this way emphasizes that Chase is the only folder of shirts while loads of washed dishes comes from both Ryan and Chase. Moving down on the social PPC, the point (20,6) can be written as (20+0,0+6). Here Chase is spending all of his time folding shirts (20) and spends no time washing dishes. Ryan continues to not fold shirts because he spends all of his time washing dishes (6). This point represents Ryan and Chase spending all their time producing the item for which they have a comparative advantage no time on the other task.

Now suppose Chase and Ryan decide they want more than 20 folded shirts. Chase is already spending all of his time folding, so any further increase in folded shirts must come from Ryan. This causes the social PPC to kink at the point (20,6), represented by point *Z* in Figure 2.2. The social PPC will now parallel Ryan's PPC. Consider the point (30,4). It could be rewritten as (20+10,0+4) to underscore that Chase is spending all of his time folding shirts (20) and Ryan is spending part of his time folding shirts (10) and part of it washing dishes (4). Continuing down the social PPC, one arrives at point *Y*, (45,1). Again, the point can be re-expressed as (20+25,0+1). Chase continues to spend all of his available time and effort on folding shirts (20) while Ryan spends most of his time folding shirts (25) for a total of 45. The number of washed loads of dishes falls to 1, which Ryan does with the limited amount of time left. Finally, one gets to the endpoint where both Ryan and Chase are spending all their time folding shirts (50) and washing zero loads of dishes. The social production possibilities curve is labeled QQ in Figure 2.2.

The social production possibilities curve now constructed possesses all the properties of the individual PPCs. Two consequences of trading become evident. First, the area of available choices expands greatly for both Chas and Ryan. Point *A* from Figure 2.1 is marked in Figure 2.2. It was an unavailable combination when Chase and Ryan relied on their individual resources. By joining forces, point *A* has changed from an unavailable point to an inefficient point. That is, from a point that seemed to Ryan, and Chase in particular, very desirable (unlimited wants) but unattainable (limited resources) to a point that does not make use of all the available resources. The change in the status of point *A* shows precisely why Ryan and Chase will engage in trade: mutually beneficial improvements in their economic opportunities. What is true for Ryan and Chase is ultimately true for all of us. Because the range and quantity of goods and services expands enormously by trading, modern economies[7] exhibit a highly developed amount of trading. No one produces a .00000003% of an iPhone, a .00000067% of some cool app, or even .0008% of a pizza. Rational, optimizing individuals specialize in activities for which they are good at (have a comparative advantage) and then trade with others to get the goods and services they desire.

The second feature of the social PPC in Figure 2.2 is it is not a smooth, straight line. It has a kink at point *Z*. Formally, Ryan's and Chase's PPCs are continuous while the social PPC is not. Recall that point *Z* is the point that production of folded shirt started to include Ryan. Ryan does not have a comparative in folded shirts so that as he allocates more time to folding shirts, the decline in loads of washed dishes is greater than for Chase. The **Rule of Increasing Opportunity Cost** indicates when the production of a good or service is increased (more folded shirts), the resources with the lowest opportunity costs should be used first (Chase), followed by the resources with the next lowest opportunity costs (Ryan), then the next lowest, and so on.

A somewhat humorous example will help. Visualize a tall farmer sitting next to an apple tree. Apples are priced at a nickel apiece. Four apples lay on the ground while most are in the tree at various heights. The two resources in this example are physical effort and exposure to injury. He has an order for four apples. The question is "In what order will the farmer gather the apples?" Applying the rule of increasing opportunity cost, he will begin with the ones on the ground. He will expend the least amount of effort and expose himself to a very small degree of risk. Suppose the farmer needs to gather six apples. His height makes it possible for him to simply reach the two apples on the lowest branch. If he needs more than six, he will have to get the ladder and climb. The actions required to gather the 7th apple demand a

---

[7] The term "modern economies" does not refer only to current economies. High degrees of complex trading have existed through the ages.

great deal more physical exertion and exposure to risk of injury. Obviously, retrieving the last apple at the very top of the tree requires the greatest amount of physical effort and the extent of injury one could experience falling from that height would be significant. The farmer is increasing the gathering of apples by getting the ones with the lowest opportunity costs, then the next lowest opportunity costs, then the next,…, until the apple at the very top of the tree, possessing the largest opportunity cost, is claimed. This is why the rule of increasing opportunity cost is also known as the ***Rule of Low Hanging Fruit.***

Large Economy, Multi-Person Production Possibilities Curve

Generalizing from an island economy populated by Ryan and Chase to a modern economy like the Unite States is not as difficult as it might seem. Suppose Zeke joins the island economy. Zeke has a comparative advantage that falls in between Chase's and Ryan's. The numerical value of Ryan's opportunity cost of a folded shirt was 0.20 and Chase's opportunity cost was 0.10. For Zeke, the opportunity cost is, say, 0.15. The social production possibilities curve will have two kinks. When increasing the production of folded shirts, Chase is still the resource with the lowest opportunity cost so he will be the first to begin folding shirts. Once Chase has allocating all of his time to folding shirt, the second lowest opportunity cost resource, Zeke, will start to fold shirts. This produces a kink in the PPC. Then, when Chase and Zeke are spending all their time folding shirts, any further increase in the production of folded shirts must come from Ryan. A second kink now appears in the social production possibilities curve, suggesting a pattern. With two people, one kink appeared; with three people, two kinks present themselves. As long as each person has a different opportunity cost, n people will produce a social production possibilities with $n - 1$ kinks. As n gets large, the kinks grow closer and closer together. For a large economy, like the U.S. economy, then the social PPC becomes a smooth, concave curve. This curve is illustrated in Figure 2.3.

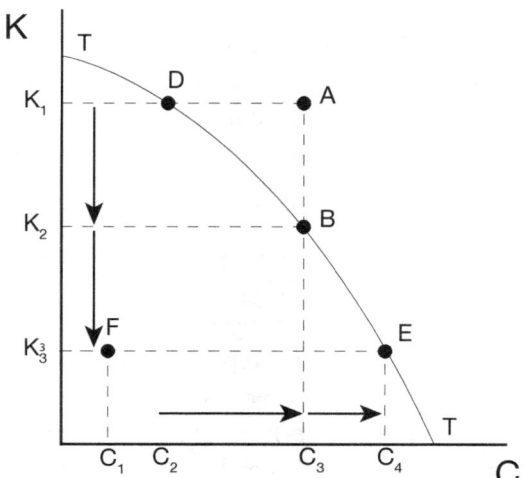

FIGURE 2.3

Rather than washed dishes and folded shirts, the many-person, large-economy production possibilities curve needs to have more realistic tasks or goods or services to consider. Societies generally are concerned with the production of two broad categories of items. *Capital goods* are man-made resources, e.g., robotics, backhoes, whiteboards, and markers. By this definition, a barrel of oil would be considered to be a capital good rather than a natural resource. In fact, the only natural resources are the ones undisturbed by man. The pool of oil in the ground is the natural resource; the minute man starts to extract it, the resources change from a natural resource to a capital good. *Consumer goods* are goods or services whose final consumption rests with the consumer. These items will never be used by a firm to produce something else. Clear examples include hamburgers, dry cleaning, and eyeglasses. Categorizing iPad's is more challenging. When a firm purchases an iPad for one of its salesman to use in the field, the iPad is a unit of capital. If that same iPad was instead purchased for a child to use for learning and entertainment, it must be a consumer good. The classification of a good or service as capital or consumer flows from how it is used, not from some rigid definition. In Figure 2.3, capital goods, labeled *K*, are measured on the vertical axis while consumer goods, labeled *C*, are quantified on the horizontal axis.

The shape of the social PPC contains the essential features as the two-person PPC. The slope is negative and the curve is concave. The negative feature results from the tradeoff inherent in scarcity. To have move consumer goods requires that society have fewer capital goods. This is illustrated in Figure 2.3 as society moves from point *D* to point *B*. At point *D*, society enjoys K_1 capital goods and C_2 consumer goods. If society decides it wants to have more consumer goods, say, C_3, the economy is certainly capable of that level of production. The increased output of consumer goods does have a cost: production of capital goods must fall. Specifically, the production of capital goods falls from K_1 to K_2. The same is true if the economy moves from point *B* to point *E*. As the economy expands the amount of consumer goods produced from C_3 to C_4, the amount of produced capital goods falls from K_2 to K_3. The concavity reflects the rule of increasing opportunity cost. The reduction in capital goods production from K_1 to K_2 is of the same size as the reduction from K_2 to K_3. But the increase in consumer goods is unequal. The first increase in consumer goods, $\Delta C^1 = (C_3 - C_2)$, is relatively large while the second increase, $\Delta C^2 = (C_4 - C_3)$, is relatively small and certainly $\Delta C^1 > \Delta C^2$. As one moves down the social PPC, more and more consumer goods are being produced. This requires more and more resources to be taken from the production of capital goods. The resources used for the production of capital that can be easily switched to the production of consumer goods will move first. As more consumer goods are produced, less easily switched resources will move from capital goods' production to consumer goods' production and thus the increase in the output of consumer goods becomes smaller.

As with the simple social PPC constructed earlier, the multi-person PPC divides the area of the graph into two regions. Point *A* in Figure 2.3 involves the combination of K units of capital and C_3 units of consumables. The economy has inadequate resources to achieve that combination of capital and consumer goods. The economy can produce K_1 units of capital goods. But if it does, only C_2 units of consumer goods are possible. Alternatively, the economy can make C_3 units of consumer goods but only K_2 pieces of capital goods can be manufactured. If a combination of capital and consumer goods rests on the production possibilities curve or exists on the interior region, then it is available. The economy is capable of producing both the level of capital goods and the level of consumer goods consistent with the combination. In Figure 2.3, combinations *D, B, E,* and *F* are all available with the economy's current resource base.

The distinction between efficient and inefficient combinations persists and is illustrated by the difference between points that lie along the PPC and those points inside the PPC. Combinations of capital and consumer goods indicated by points *D, B,* and *E* are all efficient points. Established above, these points are available. The additional feature of the points along the production possibilities curve is the entire resource base of the economy is in fact being utilized. No resource contained in the economy remains idle. This is true whether the economy is at point *D*, which contains much capital goods production and relatively little consumer goods, or at point *E*, where relatively few capital goods are made but a great deal of consumer goods are produced. Combination *F*, being in the interior of the production possibilities curve, means some part of the resource base is not being utilized. Some amount of labor or capital stands idle. The economy is operating at an inefficient point when it is at *F*.

Unlike points *D, B,* and *E*, at point *F*, the inefficient point, society can realize more capital goods and more consumer goods simultaneously . Because some part of the resource base stands idle, bringing the unemployed resources into use allows for the expanded production of both goods. Adding the idle resources to the resources already employed can cause movement from point *F* to, say, point *B*. Now the economy is at a combination of capital and consumer goods consistent with efficiency. Production of both capital and consumer goods is larger. A tradeoff did not occur. Since each and every country always has a positive amount of unemployment and some degree of disuse of man-made resources, no nation is ever operating on its PPC. One of the goals of policymakers is to move the economy from points of greater inefficiency to points of lesser inefficiency.

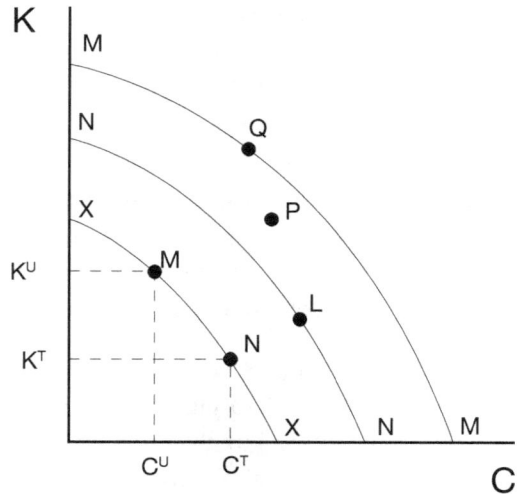

FIGURE 2.4

The above analysis refers repeatedly to an economy's resource base. The definition of the **resource base** includes the stock of existing capital equipment, the size of the labor force, and the state of technological development. Societies can therefore influence the future size of their resource base. Two countries, Uruk and Tyre are illustrated in Figure 2.4. Both of these countries have identical resources. As a result, they have identical PPC's. In Figure 2.4 the production possibilities curve label **XX** is not one but two PPC's. The production possibilities curve for Uruk and the PPC for Tyre are lying on top of each other. Additionally, the production possibilities curve **XX** is drawn based on data from 2013. The two countries are different in one noticeable way. Country Uruk picks the point labeled **M**. Point **M** indicates county Uruk is fully utilizing its resource base. It also shows a greater emphasis on the production of capital goods. Specifically, country Uruk makes K^U capital goods and C^U consumer goods. Country Tyre is making a decidedly different choice. Fully utilizing its resource base, country Tyre chooses the combination labeled **N**. Point **N** implies a combination of capital goods and consumer goods that stresses greater production of consumer goods relative to country Uruk. This must necessarily mean country Tyre is choosing to make fewer capital goods. Specifically, country Tyre produces K^T capital goods and C^T consumer goods.

Jump to the state of the two economies in 2016. Remember part of the resource base is the amount of capital equipment present in the economy. Between 2013 and 2016 some of the capital stock that was contained in the 2013 resource base of both countries has worn out and been retired. Assume the amount of retired capital was equal. The capital produced in 2013 by the two countries has been added to the 2016 resource base. Country Uruk committed more of its 2013 resource base to the production of capital goods (K^U) as compared with country Tyre (K^T). As a result, the size of Uruk's resource base in 2016 exceeds the size of country Tyre's resource base causing the production possibilities curve for Uruk to surpass the PPC for Tyre. In Figure 2.4, the PPC label **NN** is associated with Tyre in the year 2016. The one labeled **MM** is the 2016 production possibilities curve for Uruk. The ability of country Uruk to produce any combination of capital and consumer goods in 2016 is greater than Tyre. In 2013, point **P** is an unavailable combination of capital and consumer goods to both countries. In 2016, Tyre is still unable to pick point **P**. Uruk can not only succeed in producing the combination implied by point **P**, it is actually a point of inefficiency. If country Uruk picks **P**, it will experience unemployment of some of its resource base. Country Uruk's economic growth outperforms the economic growth for country Tyre.

Further suppose country Uruk continues, in 2016, to favor the production of capital goods over consumer goods, illustrated by point **Q**. It resides on the production possibilities curve **MM**, meaning Uruk is fully employing its resource base. Tyre persists in favoring consumer goods over capital, exemplified by point **L**. Point **L** shows country Tyre is also fully utilizing its resource base, operating on the production possibilities curve **NN**. In 2019, Uruk's PPC will again shift out to the northeast more so that the shift for Tyre.[8] The advantage country Uruk has over county Tyre in possible production combinations simply gets larger. Economic growth in country Uruk continues to outstrip growth in country Tyre. Clearly, the choices society

---

[8] To keep Figure 2.4 manageable, the PPCs for 2019 are not illustrated.

makes over the mix of consumer and capital goods are important in determining what the future holds for the economy and hence the society.

The answer to the question "Why do people trade" is rooted in comparative advantage. The existence of these phenomena leads individuals to concentrate on activities for which they are comparatively better. This generates a greater range of choices being available to society. And thus people trade. A simply survey of the surrounding economic environment makes clear the world contains much greater complexity than the one our friends Ryan and Chase inhabit. The next chapter, supply and demand, furthers the analysis of trading.

CHAPTER THREE:

How Do Markets Work?

In the last chapter it was determined that two rational, optimizing individuals were better off if they traded with each other. This is at least part of the reason that humans ultimately began to organize themselves into tribal societies. At the other end of the scale is the most developed form of a tribal society: civilization. Additionally, the degree of technological sophistication of the tribe or the civilization can be extensive or limited. It does not matter what dimension of human organization one considers. Any and all groupings of humans must answer the 3 following questions.

The 3 Questions

"What is going to be produced?"

"How will it be produced?"

"Who will receive what is produced?"

The specific answers given to the questions are not of concern. It is reasonable to speculate the answer to the "What is going to be produced?" question includes some amount of water, calories, and possibly shelter. The point to be made here is not about the answers that emerge but how they emerge. What process produces the answers to the three questions? Two broad approaches have evolved. The first is central planning. The answers to the three question come from above, typically from some form of governmental institution. The most extreme version of a planned economy is a command economy, where the government adopts a top-down administrative allocation of resources based on bureaucratic organization. From the end of World War II to the late 1980s, central planning was common and known as Communism. Today, examples of this mechanism are few and far between. Cuba and North Korea are the only remaining command economies, and Cuba seems to be tottering.

The alternative to central planning is a system of free markets. The remaining countries of the world practice, to a greater or lesser degree, free markets. It is also true that many countries have segments of their economies where central planning occurs. Most countries are therefore characterized as being mixed systems, combining both planning and freedom. The distinguishing feature of decision making in a free market system is that individuals provide the answers to the questions. This leads to highly decentralized decisions; the answers to the three questions come from below. Firms are formed to respond to society's answer to the "What is going to be produced" questions or to improve on the current answer to the "How will it be produced" question. The answer to the "Who will receive what is produced" question is determined, for the most part, by the distribution of income.

The Marketplace

A marketplace forms from two groups. They go by many pairs of names: buyers and sellers; consumers and firms; demanders and suppliers. At its core, a market requires someone who wants to buy something and another someone who is willing to sell the something. Both sides will be developed and then the two will be joined. The discussion will begin with buyers because everyone reading this book has purchased a multitude of goods and services.

Demand

The analysis of the marketplace starts with those who answer the "What should be produced" question. And those who answer that question are the buyers. The **Law of Demand** proposes the quantity of the good or service demanded is inversely or negatively related to the price of that good or service. Rational, optimizing individuals wish to purchase more of an item when the price is low and purchase less of it when the price is high. The formal rationalization for the relationship will be developed in a future chapter. Suffice it to say 1) millions and millions of individuals down through the ages have behaved in accordance with the law of demand and, 2) it only makes sense.

The law of demand can be expressed formally with the assistance of an equation. The **demand function** is a mathematical illustration of the law of demand. For example,

$$Q^D_X = f(P_X).$$

The equation is read as the quantity of good X demanded, represented by Q^D_X depends on the price of good X, represented by P_X. The particular good or service "X" is immaterial. Toothpaste or beer or dry cleaning; all goods and services should comply with the law of demand. A specific version of a demand function is given by:

$$Q^D_X = 5 - \tfrac{1}{2} \times P_X.$$

Inspecting the equation reveals the slope is negative, as the law of demand requires. The expression for slope is the change in the quantity of good X demanded divided by the change in the price of good X, which equals $-\tfrac{1}{2}$. Table 3.1 contains the value of quantity demanded for various prices based on the above equation. Beginning with a relatively high price of $8,

$$Q^D_X = 5 - \tfrac{1}{2} \times \$8 = 5 - 4 = 1.$$

The quantity demanded is 1 unit when the price is $8. As the price falls to $6, consumers are now willing to purchase 2 units of good X, in accordance with the law of demand.

TABLE 3.1 Demand Data	
P_X	Q^D_X
$8	1.0
$7	1.5
$6	2.0
$5	2.5
$4	3.0
$3	3.5
$2	4.0

Figure 3.1 illustrates a ***demand curve***, the graphical representation of the demand function. It is constructed from the data contained in Table 3.1 and labeled ***D***. The curve slopes downward from left to right. As the price of the good or service falls, the quantity demanded increases; as the price rises, the quantity demanded decreases.

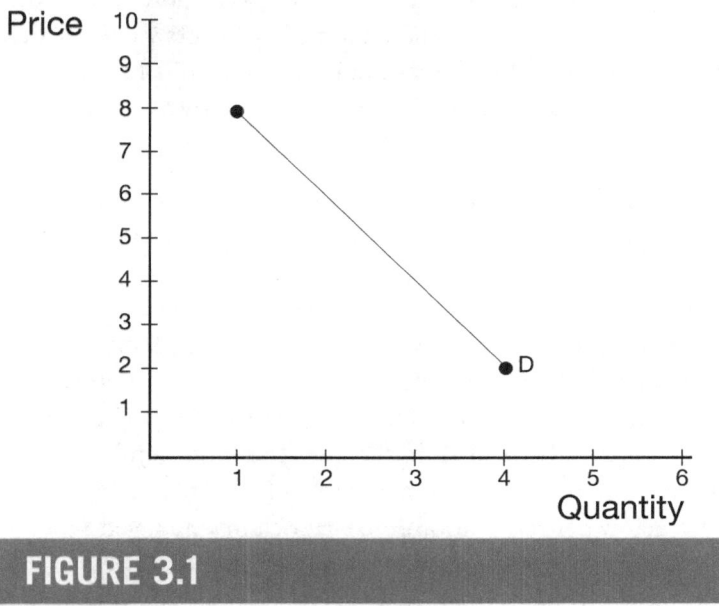

FIGURE 3.1

A point about the orientation of the graph. In the demand function above, the relationship is written with the quantity demanded as the dependent variable, as it is on the left hand side of the equals sign, while price, being on the right hand side, is taken as the independent variable. The usual procedure for graphing a function is to place the dependent variable on the vertical axis and the independent variable on the horizontal axis. In Figure 3.1, the relationship has been reversed: price is on the vertical axis and quantity demanded is on the horizontal axis. This is simply an age old convention in economics. Ultimately it will prove quite useful to have reversed the axis. In mathematical terms, the original demand function has simply been inverted. That is,

$$P_X = f^{-1}(Q^D_X).$$

For the specific equation being used, $Q^D_X = 5 - \frac{1}{2} \times P_X$, the inverse function is

$$P_X = 10 - 2 \times Q^D_X.$$

Note that

$$P_X = 10 - 2 \times 1 = 10 - 2 = 8.$$

When the quantity demanded is set to 1 unit, solving the equation for price results in $8, the same price and quantity demanded association found in Table 3.1. Hence, either way of writing the demand equation results in the same price being associated with the same quantity demanded.

The **buyer's reservation price** is the maximum price one is willing to pay for a good or service. The buyer's reservation price is not a price adopted for bargaining purposes. If the buyer's reservation price for a cup of coffee is $5, then a price of $5.01 causes no sale to occur. If the sale does occur at a price of $5.01, then $5 was not the buyer's reservation price. It must be the price at which any further increase results in a refusal to buy. In Table 3.1 or Figure 3.1, a price of $2 is associated with a quantity demanded of 4 units. If the price was any lower, more than 4 units would be demanded. If the price was any higher, fewer than 4 units would be demanded. The price of $2 defines the buyer's reservation price for 4 units for this good or service. In general, the price associated with a particular quantity of the good demanded always defines the buyer's reservation price.

An enlightening point about the behavior of rational, optimizing individuals can be made with the concept of a reservation price. It is common for people who return from shopping to show off their purchases and declare they have saved money (more accurately, income) because the store was having a sale. Since it is impossible to save income by spending income, this cannot be true. Something advantageous has, indeed, happened. Suppose Betsy liked a pair of shoes whose price was $170. Betsy's reservation price, the most she is willing to pay, sits at $100 for the shoes. No purchase is made. The next time she goes to Nordstrom's she notices that the shoes are on sale, priced at $70. She now makes the purchase because the sale price of the shoes is below her reservation price. Her claim she saved $100, the difference between the initial price and the sale price is wrong. She is experiencing an economic surplus of $30; the difference between her reservation price and the actual price paid but she has saved not a cent. So her cry "I saved money" needs to be changed to "I did not spend as much as I was willing to spend."

Supply

Those who most directly answer the "How will it be produced" question is the next topic. The **Law of Supply** indicates the relation between the quantity of good X supplied and the price of good X is positive or direct. As the price of a good or service increases, firms are willing to produce more. Chapter Six contains the exact explanation of the connection between price and the quantity supplied. Sense can still be made of the relationship with the tools already developed.

Recall the example of the apple farmer gathering apples and the rule of increasing opportunity costs in Chapter Two. The apple farmer started with the easiest apples to gather, the ones on the ground, and then moved to progressive more costly apples, the ones higher in the tree. The apples further from the ground are more costly because 1) they require more effort to get to them and 2) the severity of injury from falling out of the tree is worse. If the price of apples is low, the apple farmer has little incentive to pick any apples. The small compensation for apples induces little desire to make the effort or endure the risk of extensive apple gathering. However, as the price of apples rises, the apple farmer has a growing incentive to pick apples, easy ones first and then costly ones. The greater payment for apples gives the apple farmer a greater incentive to expend the effort and take the risk of increased apple gathering. Higher prices then cover the increased opportunity costs associated with increased production.

Explicit expression of the law of supply requires the assistance of an equation. The **supply function** is a mathematical illustration of the law of supply:

$$Q^S_X = f(P_X).$$

The equation is read as the quantity of good X supplied, represented by Q^S_X depends on the price of good X, represented by P_X. The particular good or service X is immaterial. All goods and services should comply with the law of supply. A specific version of a supply function is given by

$$Q^S_X = \tfrac{1}{2} \times P_X.$$

TABLE 3.2 Supply Data	
P_X	Q^S_X
$2	1.0
$3	1.5
$4	2.0
$5	2.5
$6	3.0
$7	3.5
$8	4.0

The slope of the above equation, the change in the quantity of good X supplied divided by the change in the price of good X, is ½. The positive sign of the slope reflects the law of supply. Table 3.2 contains the value of quantity supplied for various prices. When the price is $4, firms are willing to produce 2 units of good X. Just as the law of supply predicts, when the price is $8, quantity supplied rises to 4 units.

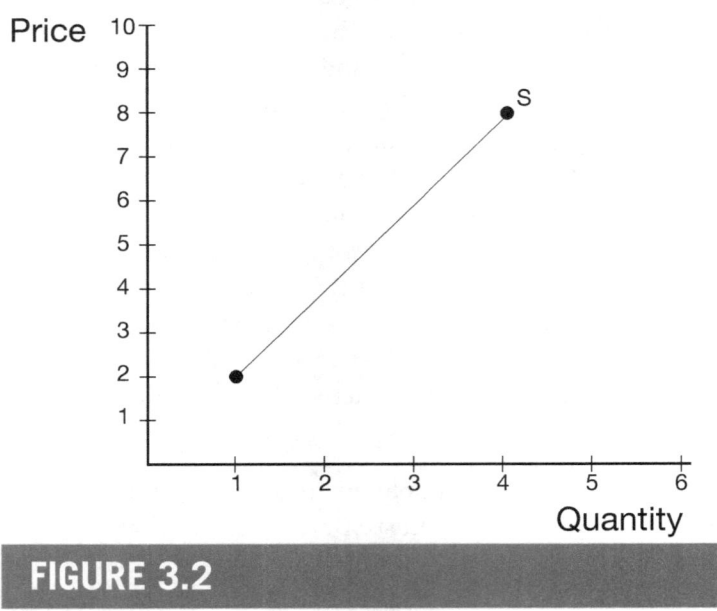

FIGURE 3.2

Figure 3.2 presents a ***supply curve***, labeled ***S***, the graphical representation of the supply function, derived from the information in Table 3.2. It slopes upward from left to right. As the price of the good or service rises, the quantity supplied increases; as the price falls, the quantity supplied decreases. As it was for the demand curve, the inverse supply curve is being graphed, i.e.,

$$P_X = 2 \times Q^S_X.$$

The supply curve reveals the ***seller's reservation price***, the minimum price firms are willing to accept to produce a good or service. For demand, the reservation price is the maximum one is willing to pay but for firms there is no limit to the maximum price they would be willing to accept ("$5, ok; $10, even better!"). For firms, there is a price below which they will not produce a given amount of output. The apple farmer needs a certain price to retrieve a given quantity of apples. From Table 3.2, the minimum price necessary to get 2 units produced is $4. If the price is greater than $4, say $8, then the first two units will definitely be produced, along with 2 additional units. The price associated with a particular quantity of the good supplied establishes the sellers' reservation price.

Equilibrium: The Market

With the initial development of demand and supply complete, the combining of the two concepts reveals the marketplace. Table 3.3 coordinates the data from Tables 3.1 and 3.2. The first column is the price of good X and ranges from $8 to $2. The second column is the quantity of good X supplied at the prices listed in the first column.

The quantity of good X demanded at the listed prices appears in the third column. The final column is quantity supplied minus quantity demanded. Figure 3.3 combines the demand curve from Figure 3.1 and the supply curve from Figure 3.2 into a graph of the marketplace.

TABLE 3.3	Market Equilibrium		
P_X	Q^S_X	Q^D_X	$Q^S_X - Q^D_X$
$8	4.0	1.0	3.0
$7	3.5	1.5	2.0
$6	3.0	2.0	1.0
$5	2.5	2.5	0
$4	2.0	3.0	−1.0
$3	1.5	3.5	−2.0
$2	1.0	4.0	−3.0

Equilibrium is a state where two competing forces reach balance so that neither overwhelms the other. In economics, supply and demand are the competing forces. Suppliers produce a lot when price of good X is high but consumers don't wish to purchase much. Looking at the first row of Table 3.3, at the price of $8, suppliers will produce 4 units but consumers only want to buy 1 unit. Obviously, not a state of equilibrium. Alternatively, demander wish to purchase much when the price of good X is low, but producers produce little at low prices. In the last row of Table 3.3, at the price of $2, consumers want to buy 4 units but producers only produce a single unit, resulting in disequilibrium. There is a price at which the desires of consumers and suppliers coincide. At the price of $5, buyers want to purchase 2.5 units and sellers wish to produce 2.5 units, achieving a state of equilibrium. The *equilibrium price, P^E_X* is the price at which quantity of good X demanded equals the quantity of good X supplied. The *equilibrium quantity, Q^E_X* is the quantity of good X which results at the equilibrium price. Figure 3.3 is a graphical representation of the data. At point E, the demand curve and the supply curve intersect at a single price, meaning quantity demanded equals quantity supplied. As long as the data for good X in the quantity supplied column and the quantity demanded column remain the same, then the equilibrium price will remain at $5 and the equilibrium quantity will stay at 2 5 units.

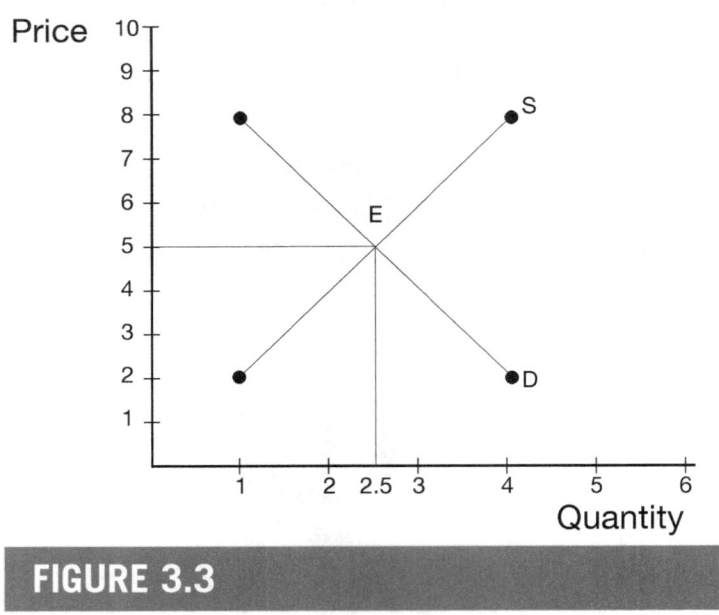

FIGURE 3.3

When discussing the condition of equilibrium it is common to misspeak. The equilibrium condition is achieved when the quantity demanded equals the quantity supplied. Alternatively, one can say the equilibrium occurs where the demand curve intersects the supply curve. What is completely incorrect to claim is equilibrium exists where demand equals supply. To say demand equals supply is to say the demand curve depicted in Figure 3.1 lies on top of the supply curve presented in Figure 3.2. Since one of them slopes downward and the other slopes upwards, they can never be the same. The other way to conceive the phrase supply equals demand is to put the supply curve on top of the demand curve, which is equally invalid. At the equilibrium, the quantity demanded, a point on the demand curve equals the quantity supplied, a point on the supply curve. The demand curve, a function, does not equal the supply curve, a different function. To speak of the demand and supply curve themselves, one must say the point at which they intersect. Additionally, do not suggest that demand exceeds supply. That would be to say the demand curve is so far to the right to not share a point of intersection with the supply curve. The same impossibility holds when one says supply exceeds demand. Quantity demanded can certainly exceed quantity supplied and vice versa and that is the next topic.

The market will not start at an equilibrium, requiring an examination of the marketplace's adjustment process. Looking at both Table 3.3 and Figure 3.4, prices $8, $7, & $6 are all above the equilibrium price of $5, which must cause a state of disequilibrium. At the price of $8, suppliers, reacting favorably to the relatively high price, produce 4 units, almost twice the equilibrium amount. Buyers, who disdain the relatively high price, wish to purchase only 1 unit. The situation is one of ***surplus or excess supply*** where the price is such that quantity supplied exceeds quantity demanded[1]. At the $8 price, the extent of the surplus is 3 units as calculated in the first row of Table 3.3. The market is plainly out of balance. Notice buyers are *content* with the circumstances at an $8 price: they wish to purchase 1 unit and indeed they are able to purchase 1 unit. Are buyers *happy* with the $8 price? Of course not. For

---

[1] Note again the difference: supply does not exceed demand; quantity supplied exceeds quantity demanded.

any and all goods and services, buyers should always prefer a lower price to a higher price. But happiness is not the issue. The issue is if buyers have a reason to alter their behavior when the price is $8. The answer is they do not. Suppliers have a very different mindset. They are *not* content, much less happy, with the outcome when the price is $8 because 3 units remain unsold. Holding the 3 units as inventory is either costly, e.g., ice cream or impossible, e.g., bananas. Suppliers have an incentive to change their behavior to eliminate the excess inventory. Specifically, they will start to cut the price of the good. Suppose they cut it to $7.

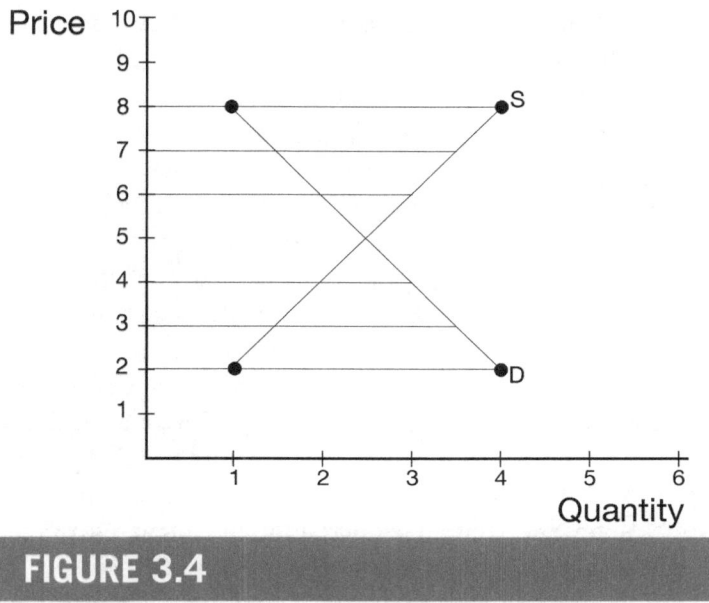

FIGURE 3.4

At a price of $7, the degree of disequilibrium in the market is smaller. The lowering of the price sets off two effects which serve to lessen the surplus. The lowering of the price causes the quantity supplied to fall from 4 to 3.5 units in accordance with the law of supply. This alone would have reduced the surplus. The price cut also causes an increase in the quantity demanded, rising from 1 unit to 1.5 reflecting the law of demand and, by itself, would have lessen the surplus. Taken together, Table 3.3 shows the surplus shrinks from 3 units to 2 units. For the same reasons discussed above, buyers are content with the circumstances at a $7 price but sellers are not. Having reduced but not eliminated the surplus by lowering price, sellers will lower price again. At the $6 price, the degree of disequilibrium is smaller still. Quantity supplied is now 3 units while quantity demanded is 2 units, resulting in a 1 unit surplus. Balance in the market has almost been established.

How will supplier know to stop lowering price? It is tempting to say "when they reach the equilibrium price of $5." However, if suppliers knew $5 was the equilibrium price they presumably would have started there. Suppliers know to stop cutting price when the circumstance that caused them to start cutting price abates. When quantity supplied equals quantity demanded, the surplus is zero, the market is in equilibrium and firms no longer find it necessary to lower price.

Examining Figure 3.4, at the price of $8 a line segment extends from the price axis to the supply curve. Where the line segment crosses the demand curve is the relevant quantity demand, i.e., the amount buyers want at an $8 price, which is 1 unit. Where it meets the supply curve quantifies the extent of quantity supplied at 4 units. The portion of the line segment between the two curves measures the surplus. As the price falls to $6, a new line segment extends from the price axis to the supply curve. The distance between the point on the demand curve and the supply again measured the size of the surplus, which has reduced. When the $5 price is reached, the surplus is zero and equilibrium has been established.

When the price is below the equilibrium value, the marketplace is also out of balance. Returning to Table 3.3, when the price is $2, a relatively low price, buyers want to purchase 4 units. Firms wish not to manufacture much, with a quantity supplied of 1 unit. The market is in a state of **shortage or excess demand** where quantity demanded is larger than quantity supplied. At the $2 price, the extent of the shortage is 3 units.[2] Shortages reverse the roles of the buyers and sellers. At the $2 price, sellers are content with the outcome. They produced 1 unit and it was sold. Firms would, of course, prefer to see a higher price but the current situation does not lead them to change their behavior. Consumers, alternatively, are not content with the outcome. Buyers want to purchase 4 units but only 1 unit is available. Reviewing the third column of Table 3.3, note someone is willing to pay $8 to get 1 unit of the good. Apparently, that someone values this good a great deal and will act to ensure they get the 1 unit produced. What is their solution? The person with the $8 reservation price will start to bid up the price. eBay provides an excellent example of the adjustment process. An item is offered for auction at a given price. To keep the example manageable, the item has no reservation price or "buy now" option. Assuming multiple people are interested in buying the item, a process of bidding begins. Ultimately the price begins to rise as people outbid each other. The winner of the auction is the one who bids the highest price and presumably has the highest reservation price.

Suppose the price is bid up to $4. The quantity supplied rises to 2 units while quantity demanded falls to 3 units. The shortage has decreased from 3 units to 1 unit, meaning the degree of disequilibrium is relatively small. However, some buyer still has an incentive to call out a higher price because the market is short 1 unit. The bidding up of the price will cease when quantity supplied equals quantity demanded or the shortage equals zero. If buyers knew that $5 was the equilibrium price, they would have jumped to it immediately.

To verify the transition of understanding from table to graph, refer to Figure 3.4 again. At the price of $2, a line segment extends from the price axis to the demand curve. Where the line crosses the supply curve shows the quantity supplied when the price is $2 to be 1 unit. Continuing to the right along the line, when the demand curve is reached, the quantity demanded is quantified as 4 units. The portion of the line segment between the supply curve and the demand curve is the extent of the shortage. At a price of $2, the shortage is 3 units. When the price is bid up to $4, the

---

[2] For the surplus, the different between quantity supplied and quantity demanded is an observable number; 4 units were produced, 1 unit was purchased leaving 3 unsold units. In the case of a shortage, quantity demanded is 4 units and quantity supplied is 1 unit. The 4 units of quantity demanded do not exist as observable items, the 1 unit produced is observable. It will be maintained that the subtraction-the shortage- can be made even if it is not truly observable.

line segment in between the supply and demand curve continues to measure the shortage, which is now only 1 unit. Finally, when a price of $5 is reached, the shortage is eliminated and equilibrium is established.

The above analysis shows the marketplace is **stable**: if price is something other than the equilibrium price, forces in the market will move the price towards its equilibrium value. If price is above the equilibrium value, firms acting in accordance with their incentives, will drive the price down to the equilibrium. If price is below the equilibrium, buyers, acting in their self-interest, will push the price up to the equilibrium value. In reality, markets rarely locate the equilibrium price. The important conclusion to remember is markets are always adjusting towards a state of equilibrium.

Determinates of Supply and Demand

The discussion of demand and supply has, for clarity, been severely restricted and simplified. Price is obviously not the only factor influencing the quantity demanded or the quantity supplied of any particular good or service. The next two sections release the simplifications made in the previous section and explore other variables which shape supply and demand and ultimately the marketplace.

Demand

The discussion of demand will now inject factors other than the price of the good or service. Recall the demand function introduced earlier:

$$Q^D_X = f(P_X).$$

The task here adds more variables to the equation. The first additional variable to include is income, denoted by a capital I. Mathematically, the demand function has been expanded as follows:

$$Q^D_X = f(P_X, I).$$

Income can be more important than price in some demand situations. For example, when purchasing a home, the procedure is to first establish how much house one can afford. This evaluation is based on one's past, current, and future income. After the assessment, the amount that will be loaned is announced and then a search for a home commences. At this point, changes in the price of a specific home or the housing market as a whole can affect the purchase. But one does not begin the process by looking at housing prices. At the other end of the spectrum, for some goods, income is likely irrelevant in deciding how much to purchase. Toothpicks come to mind. Most goods and services should fall in between i.e., income is an important but secondary factor determining how much will be purchased.

The influence of income on demand takes one of two directions. A **normal good** is a good or service for which demand increases when income increases. If income falls, then demand for a normal good falls. Most goods and services possess this characteristic. It is convenient to think of the increase in demand as an increase in the number of units. Realistically, this view is not applicable to all goods or services.

Suppose a college student owns a car with significant wear and tear. The student then graduates and gets a good paying job, which means his income has increased. Does this mean he will now purchase two more used cars with significant wear and tear? Highly improbable. The more likely outcome is he will buy a new car or a slightly used one. It is certainly true that "buying more" means "buying better" in many, but not all, circumstances.

An *inferior good* is one where demand increases when incomes fall. Similarly, when incomes rise, the demand for an inferior good falls. Ramen noodles likely qualify. Suppose the above mentioned college student consumed a great deal of ramen noodles in college because they are inexpensive and easy to prepare. After spending 5 years in college and eating Ramen noodles, when he graduates and his income swells, he decides to never eat ramen noodle ever again. Thus, a decrease in demand. If, sadly, the student loses his first job and his income falls, he returns to his inexpensive hot meal of ramen noodles. Hence, an increase in demand. This is also an excellent time to point out one man's meat is another man's poison. That is, some college students may love ramen noodles so for them they are a normal good. No absolute rule exists to determine which goods are normal and which are inferior

The next variable to place in the demand equation is the price of other goods and services, signified by P_{OG}. If one were to randomly grab two items in one's apartment, it is unlikely any relation would exist. Consumption of toilet bowl cleaner does not influence the level of baloney consumption. For some goods and services, however, there is a clear relationship. A new good, Z, with a price of P_Z, joins good X for the discussion. The first category is *substitutes*, goods or services used in place of one another. Original crackers or whole wheat crackers? Heinz ketchup or Hunt's ketchup? iPhone or Windows phone? And the age old question, Coke or Pepsi? For goods X and Z to be substitutes, when the price of good Z, increases, the demand for good X increases. Likewise, if P_Z falls, demand for good X will fall. Take jeans for example. Both Lee jeans and Levis jeans fulfill, more or less, the desire to wear a certain kind of pants, i.e., they can be used in place of one another. A decline in the price of Lee brand jeans will lead to a decrease in the demand for Levi's brand jeans. As Lee jeans become less expensive, Levi's become more expensive. The quantity of Lee jeans demanded will rise and, since one uses either Lees or Levi's, the demand for Levi's jeans will fall.

The second category is *complements*: when two goods or services are used together. Peanut butter and jelly. Automobiles and gasoline (or maybe electricity). Chips and dips. For goods X and Z to be complements, when the price of good Z falls, demand for good X increases. When the price of Z falls, more of Z will be consumed. At the same time, more of a complementary good X, will also be consumed. Likewise, if the price of good Z rises and demand for good X falls, then X and Z are complements. If the price of peanut butter increases, the quantity of peanut butter demanded falls. Since people frequently consume peanut butter and jelly together, then consuming less peanut butter means less jelly is required, decreasing the demand for jelly.[3]

---

[3] The example of strongest complementary rests with left shoes and right shoes. To sell left and right shoes as a pair is not due to some legal requirement. One could sell shoes separately. Buyers select the same pattern and size of shoe for the right foot as for the left, seemingly without exception. Thus, one purchases a pairs of pumps, a left foot pump and a right foot pump.

Other variables can be included in the demand function as circumstances warrant. For example, expectations over the future price of good X could be included. If one expects P_X to rise in the future, one would want to purchase more good X today, which amounts to an increase in demand for good X. This would be an important factor to include, for example, in the demand for orange juice concentrate. If a freeze in Florida that kills some of the crop, then oranges will become more expensive in the future and consequently, the price of orange juice concentrate rises. Orange juice concentrate can be stockpiled, so one should buy more today to escape the future price increase. The analysis applies less well to demand for fresh oranges because they are unsuited to stockpiling. Tastes and preferences also affect the demand for goods and services. For goods like electricity and applesauce, tastes and preferences are unlikely to shift radically. For fad items, like the hottest Christmas toy, the expansion of demand can only be attributed to tastes changing volcanically. Soon thereafter, tastes change again, the toy becomes yesterday's newspapers, and demand drops off. How much do people fight over Bratz Dolls in 2013 as compared to 2001?

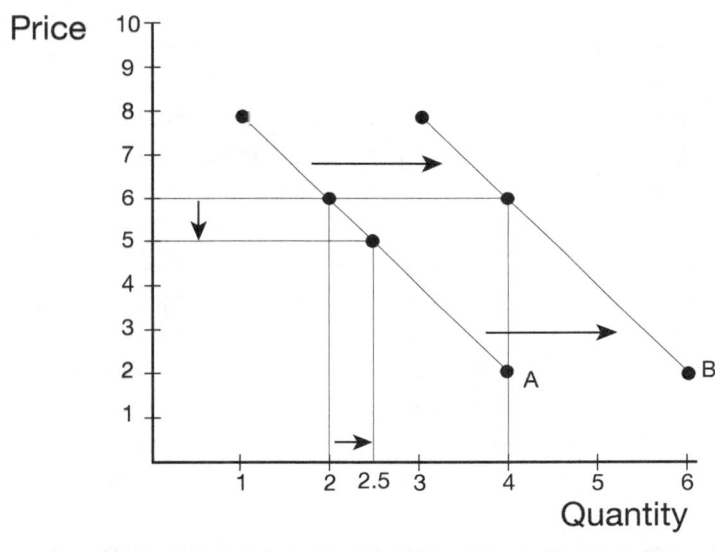

FIGURE 3.5

An important distinction needs amplification. In the first section on demand, the phrase "change in quantity demanded" was used repeatedly. In the section above, the phrase "change in demand" frequently appears. One might be tempted to assume the two phrases refer to the same type of behavior but they do not. When the price of good X increases, there is a decrease in the quantity demanded of good X; a price reduction for good X leads to an increase in the quantity demanded. More compactly, a change in the price of a good results in a change in the quantity demanded of the good. Looking at Figure 3.5, on the demand curve labeled *A*, when the price of good X falls from $6 to $5, the quantity demanded rises from 2 units to 2.5 units. One has moved from one price/quantity combination to another one. The alternative phrase to use when the price of a good changes is a "movement along a demand curve," a description reflecting the graphical interpretation shown in Figure 3.5.

TABLE 3.4	An Increase in Demand	
P_X	Q^D_X	Q^{D*}_X
$8	1.0	3.0
$7	1.5	3.5
$6	2.0	4.0
$5	2.5	4.5
$4	3.0	5.0
$3	3.5	5.5
$2	4.0	6.0

When one of the determinants of demand change, a change in demand results. At each and every price, the amount buyers want to purchase changes when income, prices of related goods, etc., change. Perusing Table 3.4, the first two columns contain the original information on price and quantity demanded. The third column has the data for an increase in demand. Suppose good X is a normal good and the incomes of consumers rise. Because buyers have more income available to spend, the amount they want to purchase expands, regardless of level of the current price of good. That said, demand curves still slope downwards. At the relatively high price of $8, buyers wished to purchased but a single unit before incomes increase. Income then increases, stimulating greater purchases: quantity demanded at $8 is now 3 units. While the income increase caused consumers to buy more, the amount is still not very large. At the other end of the demand curve, price is relatively low and quantity demanded is correspondingly larger. At the price of $2, the quantity demanded is noticeably larger than at the $8 price: 4 units versus 1 unit. After the increase in income, buyers again wish purchase more. The third column reveals demand for good X jumped from 4 to 6 units. Therefore, buyers still buy more when the price is low and less when it is high even after their incomes increase. The end result is the relationship between price and quantity demanded is preserved but the specific quantity demanded associated with a specific price has shifted. In Figure 3.5, the demand curve labeled *A* is the original demand curve and demand curve *B* is the demand curve after the increase in income. The demand curve has shifted to the right of where it was initially. At the price of $6, buyers wish to purchase 4 units; at the $5 price they wish to purchase 4.5 units. That is, at each and every price, more will be purchased. If good X had been an inferior good, the increase in incomes would have led to a decrease in demand. The values of quantity demanded associated with various prices would then be smaller rather than larger. Demand would have decreased meaning the demand curve would have shifted to the left. At each and every price buyers now want less. The terminology of demand shifting to the right or left reflects the graphical interpretation.

Both examples of an increase and a decrease in demand were based on a change in income. Changes in any of the determinants of demand cause a shifting of the demand curve to either the left or the right. As discussed above, a decrease in the price of a good that substitutes for good X will result in a decrease in demand for good X. The demand curve for good X must then shift inwards to the left. A decrease in the price of a good used with good X, a complement, leads to an increase in demand for good X and thus the demand curve for good X must shift to the right; more of good X purchased at each and every price.

Supply

The supply function can also be augmented with additional variables to reflect a more complete picture of the sellers' side of the market. The variable of greatest importance is ***technology***. An improvement in technology serves to raise the efficiency of production, thereby lowering costs. Returning to the apple farmer, suppose that currently, if he wants to pick apples that he cannot reach on his own, he must climb the tree. This is a relatively slow and dangerous method for gathering apples. He therefore requires a relatively high price to gather apples beyond his reach. Technological innovation occurs and the result is a ladder. The ladder allows the apple farmer to get to the apples higher up in the tree more easily and more safely. The greater easy and lessening of risk changes the relationship between the price of apples and quantity supplied. At a constant price for apples, the apple farmer will be willing to gather more apples by climbing higher in the tree because the ladder reduces the effort and increases the safety of apple picking. Therefore, improvement in technology cause supply to increase.

The term "technological change" raises several side issues. First, it is unclear how to measure technological change. When one analyzes a price change, measurement is clear and direct. Let the price of a good increase from $9.67 to $11.11 and another good's price increase from $3.92 to $5.36. The two price increases are of the same magnitude, $1.44, and thus can be directly compared. Technology does not have natural units of measurement. For example, is the effect on efficiency the same if more computers of older technology are added or if fewer computers of newer technology are added? As a result, comparisons of technological change between industries or even firms is more art than skill. Second, what is meant by technological change? Most people would probably say "a new machine" if asked what constitutes technological change. Does "new machine" mean a new unit of an existing piece of capital equipment or an improved version of an existing piece of capital equipment or does it mean a piece of capital equipment that did not exist before? Clearly, all three types should be considered part of technological change. A new machine, however defined, is, not the only type of technological change. Improvements in the organization of existing capital equipment require inclusion in the scope of technological change. Henry Ford did not invent the assembly line method of production or the standardization of parts. His insight, for which he was handsomely rewarded, was the application of the assembly line production methods and standardization of parts would significantly reduce the costs of producing an automobile.[4] While improvements in the organization of existing capital is less obvious, it has been responsible for considerable economic growth. The third point involves symmetry. For all the determinants of demand, one could investigate increases and decreases. Incomes go up, incomes go down; prices go up, prices go down. In the case of technological change, does it ever decrease? Would firms in an industry knowingly adopt a technological change understanding efficiency will reduce? Hard to fathom. Firms do make mistakes and adopt technologies they believe will improve their

---

[4] http://en.wikipedia.org/wiki/Assembly_line

efficiency only to realize it has actually retarded productivity. Technological change is not symmetric; it only shifts the supply curve to right.

Another variable to introduce into the supply function is the **price of inputs**, e.g., the wage rate, rent for office space, the price of electricity. If the price of the resources used to produce a good rises, then firms will be less inclined to produce. Thus, when the wage rate increases, the supply curve shifts to the left and supply has decreased. When rent for office space falls, the supply curve shifts to the right.

Finally, the **number of firms** requires inclusion in the supply function. If the number of firms in an industry increases, then at each and every price production expands. Supply will experience a rightward shift. A decline in the number of firms would serve to reduce production at every price and cause supply to decrease. The role of the determinates of supply will receive much greater scrutiny in Chapter Six.

A major distinction also exists between the term "change in quantity supplied" and "change in supply." When the price of a good or service changes, a change in quantity supplied occurs. On the supply curve, one moves from one specific price/quantity combination to another. In Figure 3.6, as the price rises from $4 to $5, producers are given a greater inducement to produce. Specifically, quantity supplied increases from 2 units to 2.5 units. If the price had fallen from $5 to $4, then quantity supplied would have declined from 2.5 units to 2 units. The movement between 2 units and 2.5 units constitutes a change in quantity supplied. On the other hand, if the state of technology improves, firms find it desirable to produce more at each and every price. In Figure 3.6, the shift from supply curve **M** to the supply curve **N** shows the increased willingness to produce output due to the improvement in technology. When the price of good X was $5 and firms had the original level of technology, they produced 2.5 units. After the technological change, firms raise production to 4.5 units at the $5 price. When any of the determinants of supply change, it generates a change in supply and the entire supply curve shifts to either the left or right.

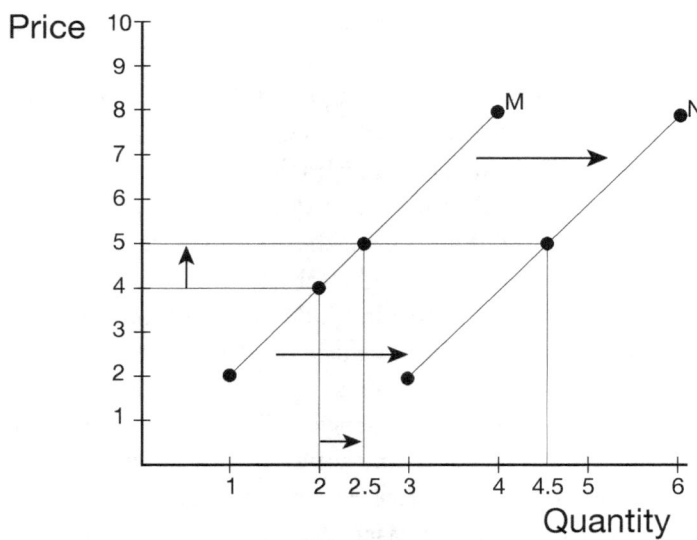

FIGURE 3.6

A warning about the way to shift the demand curve or the supply curve in the graph. Both supply and demand shift either to the left or the right. They do not shift up or down. For demand, shifting up and down versus right or left will produce the correct answer. That is, shifting demand down to show a decrease produces the same association between quantity demanded and price as does shifting demand to the left. Shifting demand up to demonstrate an increase in demand will also produce the correct association between price and quantity demanded. Unfortunately, for supply, shifting up and down does not result in the correct association between price and quantity supplied. Shifting the supply curve up to show an increase will produce associations between price and quantity supplied consistent with a reduction in supply. Likewise, shifting the supply curve down to illustrate a decrease in supply will result in associations between price and quantity supplied indicative of an increase in supply. Shift the curves left and right and the correct movement will always occur.[5]

Comparative Statics and Applications of the Market Model

Development of the basic elements of the marketplace is finished. With the model of the marketplace and equilibrium, questions about events in the economy can be addressed. The term comparative statics sounds impressive and difficult. People use comparative statics reasoning constantly. The procedure of comparative statics contains three steps. The first step is to examine how the world is now. The sidewalk is dry; the conversation is dull; the price is $5. The second step is to allow some event to occur. It rains; a charming person joins the conversation; demand changes. The third step is to observe what the world looks like after the event. The sidewalk is now wet, the conversion is now interesting; the price is no longer $5. The difficulty people experience when engaged in this reasoning is they are unable to hold all other factors constant and thus form faulty conclusions. Someone washed their car; the topic changed; supply changed. In the textbook, all other factors can be held constant and the event in the second step is solely responsible for how the world looks in the third step. This is known as ensuring all other possible influences are ***ceteris paribus*** which is Latin for "all other things being equal."

---

[5] To ensure one's understanding, refer back to Figures 3.5 and 3.6 and try shifting demand and supply up and down versus right and left.

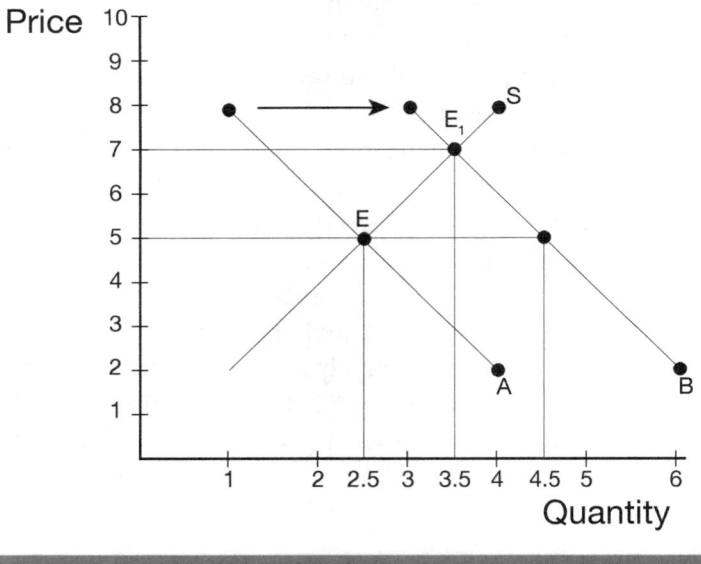

FIGURE 3.7

The first example of using the comparative statics reasoning combines a change in demand while supply is constant. The information in Figure 3.7 reflects the circumstances. Established earlier in Figure 3.3, the equilibrium price and quantity are $5 and 2.5 units. In Figure 3.7 the initial equilibrium occurs at point *E*, the intersection of the supply curve, denoted *S*, and the original demand curve, denoted *A*. Taking note of the starting equilibrium values, step one has been accomplished. Step two, the event, can now be specified. One of the determinants of demand has changed, resulting in an increase in demand which is illustrated by the demand curve labeled *B*. It matters not which determinant of demand has changed, only that demand has increased. That said, it still is useful to review the changes that move the demand curve to the right. If good X is a normal good, then an increase in income will shift demand to the right. A decrease in income coupled with good X being an inferior good would also cause the shift from *A* to *B*. An increase in the price of a substitute good or a decrease in the price of a complementary good also qualifies. Whatever the reason, demand has increased while supply has not changed. After the increase in demand, buyers want to purchase more at each and every price, including the equilibrium price of $5. Figure 3.7 reveals buyers now wish to buy 4.5 units, up from the 2.5 units previously. Sellers continue to produce 2.5 units, unaware of the increase in demand. A shortage ensues, causing a disequilibrium condition. Earlier analysis demonstrated a shortage's elimination rests with buyers. They begin a process of bidding the price of good X up. As the price climbs, sellers have greater incentive to produce. At the same time, some buyers find the new price exceeds their reservation price and withdraw from the marketplace. Ultimately, a new equilibrium establishes itself where quantity demanded equals quantity supplied or where the new demand curve, *B*, intersects the supply curve, *S*. Figure 3.7 shows the new equilibrium price is $7 and the new equilibrium quantity is 3.5 units, marked E_1 in the graph. All other determinates of demand and supply have been held constant, meaning no other factor contaminates the finding. The conclusion, the third step in the process, is an increase in demand with static supply leads to a higher equilibrium price and a larger equilibrium quantity. The result holds in reverse: a decrease in demand wedded to a constant supply curve results in a lower equilibrium price and a smaller equilibrium quantity.

The model of the marketplace predicts a greater desire for a good or service results in more of the good or service becoming available. The end result of the increase in demand is now 3.5 units are exchanged, up from the original 2.5 units. However, the increase in production does not come for free. Sellers require an inducement to produce more. Unsurprisingly, the necessary inducement is a higher price. The marketplace operates in a desirable but costly way. A point to remember.

It is helpful to again confront one's understanding of "change in quantity demanded/supplied" versus "change in demand/supply." In Figure 3.7, there has been a "increase in demand" because the demand curve shifted to the right. The ensuing shortage drives the price up, causing an "increase in quantity supplied." The movement is illustrated in Figure 3.7 by the change from the quantity supplied at point E to the quantity supplied at point E_1 along the supply curve, S. Refrain from uttering "supply increased." It did not. Quantity supplied increased.

The next case inverts the circumstances. Demand will remain constant while supply will shift. The data for the exercise is graphed in Figure 3.8. The first step of the comparative statics exercise again requires noting the original equilibrium values. Specifically, the equilibrium price is $5 and the equilibrium quantity is 2.5 units; point E in the graph. As illustrated in Figure 3.8, supply has increased from M to N. At each and every price, sellers are willing to produce more. The increase in supply is the event in the second step of the analysis. Why the supply curve shifted to the right is immaterial. Possibly an improvement in the technology the firms use. Maybe the price of some input firms use in producing their output has fallen. The reason why supply has increased does not influence the conclusions reached in the comparative statics analysis.

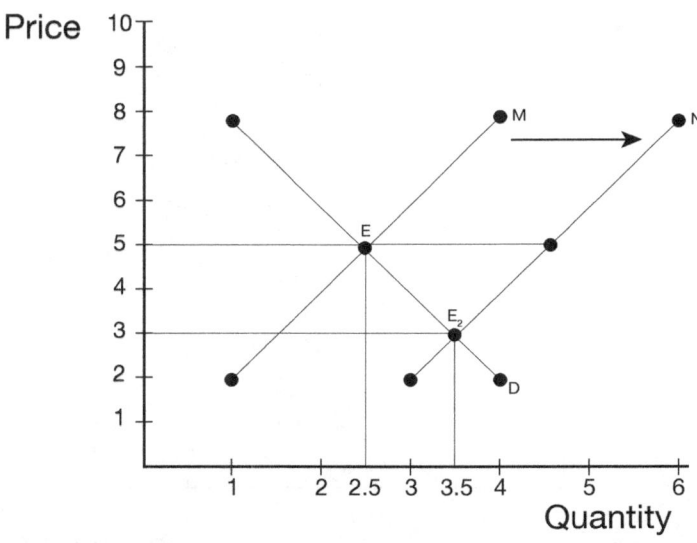

FIGURE 3.8

The graph in Figure 3.8 shows after the increase in supply, a disequilibrium condition exists. At the $5 price, firms are now willing and able to produce 4.5 units. Buyers still wish to purchase only 2.5. A surplus engulfs the market. Recall firms react to a surplus by lowering the price until the surplus dissipates. In Figure 3.8, the intersection of the new supply curve, **N**, and demand curve **D** illustrates the new equilibrium, point E_2. Specifically, the new equilibrium price is $3 and the new equilibrium quantity is 3.5. Observing the change in the equilibrium values constitutes the third step of the comparative statics logic. An increase in supply with demand constant results in a lower equilibrium price and a larger equilibrium quantity. A decrease in supply with demand unchanged would result in a higher equilibrium price and a smaller equilibrium quantity. One can count on the conclusion if *ceteris paribus* holds.[6]

It is worthwhile to note the circumstances of increased supply with demand constant produces an outcome most favorable to the buyer. The price of the good or service is lower and quantity of the available is greater. It is hard to think of a better outcome for consumers. Alternatively, the opposite circumstance, a leftward shift in supply with constant demand, brings about a higher price and a smaller quantity. Most buyers would characterize that outcome as unfortunate.

The final case allows both supply and demand to shift simultaneously. Figure 3.9 looks notably different from Figures 3.7 and 3.8. When both demand and supply shift it is impossible to make complete predictions without further information. The magnitudes of the shifts must be known. In the first case (when demand increased with constant supply), it matters not how small or big the increase in demand is, the equilibrium price will rise and the equilibrium quantity will also grow. The second case indicated is when supply increases with constant demand, the equilibrium price will fall and the equilibrium quantity enlarges; a conclusion independent of the size of the supply shift. But when both start shifting then size really does matter.

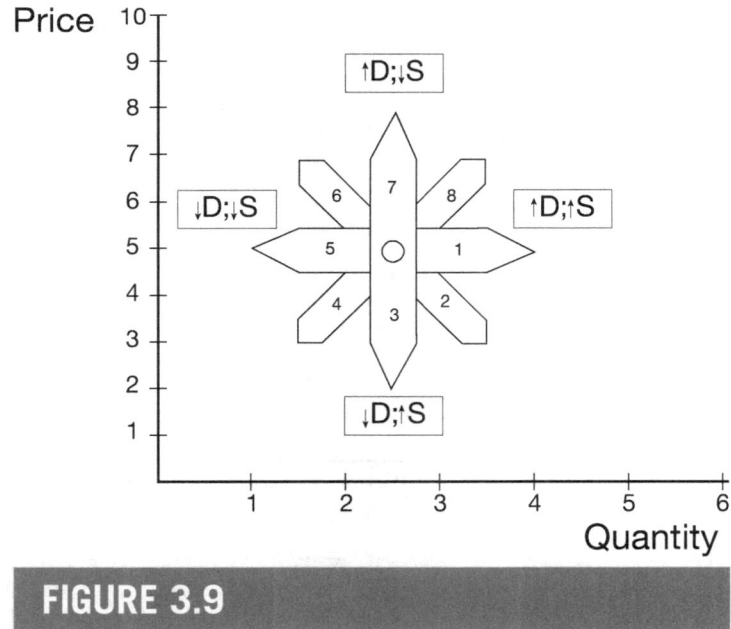

FIGURE 3.9

[6] The reader should test their comprehension of which type of change occurred to demand and which type of change occurred to supply.

42   **Chapter 3**   How Do Markets Work?

The construction of Figure 3.9 is as follows: the circle in the center of the graph represents an intersection of a supply and demand curve and hence a point of equilibrium. This is step one of the comparative statics procedure. The arrows indicate which way the supply and demand curves have shifted and are numbered 1 to 8. For example, the arrow labeled 1 and pointed due right is the circumstance of both supply and demand increasing. This is step two of the process. Since the two curves shifted to the right, the new intersection, the new equilibrium, must exist somewhere to the right of the initial equilibrium point. With a new equilibrium to the right of the initial one, it must be the case the new equilibrium quantity is to the right of the original equilibrium quantity and is larger. The change in the equilibrium price defies prediction. According to Arrow 1, it appears the equilibrium price is unchanged; the new intersection is due east of the starting point. However, the rightward shifts could resemble Arrow 8, coming to rest to the northeast of the original equilibrium. The outcome now would be the equilibrium quantity had expanded and the equilibrium price had risen. It is also possible the rightward shifts could have ended up to the southeast of the original equilibrium, shown by Arrow 2. Again, the new equilibrium quantity would be larger but the equilibrium price would have fallen relative to its starting value. Without information on the size of the rightward shifts, it is impossible to predict the outcome for the equilibrium price. The third step is thus: when demand and supply both increase, the equilibrium quantity must increase but the equilibrium price can be larger, smaller, or the same and therefore unpredictable. When both supply and demand decrease or shift to the left, as illustrated by Arrow 5, the same predicament presents itself. It is beyond doubt the equilibrium quantity is to the left of its original value, i.e., smaller. The equilibrium price can still be one of three possibilities: higher (Arrow 6), lower (Arrow 4) or constant (Arrow 5). The size of the shifts is needed to establish which of the three outcomes prevail.

When the demand and supply curve change in opposite ways, the new equilibrium will be above or below the original point of equilibrium. When supply decreases or shifts to the left and demand increases or shifts to the right, the new point of equilibrium will be somewhere above the current equilibrium point. The equilibrium price must therefore be higher. It is impossible to move above the original point and not have the equilibrium price be greater. Unfortunately, the same definitiveness does not extend to the equilibrium quantity. Its value is unpredictable without more information. If the movement is to the northwest (Arrow 6), then the equilibrium quantity will be smaller. If the new intersection is to the northeast of the original intersection (Arrow 8), equilibrium quantity will grow. If the movement is due north (Arrow 7) then the equilibrium quantity remains the same. To locate below the original equilibrium, the supply curve must shift to the right while the demand curve shifts to the left. The equilibrium price must fall relative to the original price but the change in the equilibrium quantity is unknown. It could be either larger (Arrow 2), smaller (Arrow 4), or unchanged (Arrow 3).

The third case, when both curve shift, is the most challenging and least satisfying. The model can only predict the effect for the equilibrium price or the equilibrium quantity but not both. Furthermore, which of the two equilibrium values cannot be predicted depends on the combination of demand and supply curve shifts. The hope is a comparative statics exercise will provide a full set of definitive answers but many times it does not. The third case is an excellent example of why economist frequently say "it depends." If the graph shows the exact size of the shifts, then one can say what happens to equilibrium values.

The analysis of how the basic supply and demand model works is now complete. It is surprising just how far one can get in understanding using the model of the free marketplace. An old and not overly funny joke about economics goes like this:

How do you make an Economist?

You teach a parrot to say "Supply and Demand; Supply and Demand; Supply and Demand"

The next chapter explores why buyers react differently to a change in the price of electricity and the price of Levi's jeans. It is not because one is a necessity and the other is not.

CHAPTER FOUR:

How Much Less Do I Buy When the Price Rises?

The last chapter developed a simple yet descriptive model of the interaction between suppliers and demanders. This chapter will explore the nature of demand in greater detail. Specifically, when the price of some good or service rises, do buyers purchase a sizable amount less or just a little bit less? How responsive is demand to a change in price? Aside from being an interesting question in and of itself, the answer has important implications for both private firms and governmental policies.

The discussion of elasticity requires the development of several analytical tools. In the development, one may have a tendency to lose sight of the whole point of formulating the tools. One may not be able to see the forest for the trees, i.e., by focusing on the development of the tools, the major idea may be lost. The graph in Figure 4.1 summaries the entire point of Chapter Four. Figure 4.1 contains two different demand curves for good X. The name of good X does not matter. One of the demand curves, labeled D_A, is relatively steep; the absolute value of its slope is a relatively large number. The other demand relationship, labeled D_B, is relatively flat, indicative of a slope for which the absolute value is a relatively small number. At the price of P_1, both demand curves indicate Q_1, the quantity demanded, is the same.[1] When the price rises to P_2, both demand curve show quantity demanded contracting, consistent with the Law of Demand. No one is surprised buyers want to purchase less. The interesting point, the purpose of this chapter, is that the extent of the reduction is noticeably different. For D_A, quantity demanded falls to Q_{2A} (the subscript "2A" is read as the quantity demanded at the second price for the demand curve A). This amounts to a relatively small reduction, $(Q_{2A} - Q_1)$. For D_B, quantity demanded declines to Q_{2B}. The decrease in quantity demand is substantially larger at $(Q_{2B} - Q_1)$. Developing measurements to formalize and summarize the difference between D_A and D_B and then applying the measures to decision making marks the work of this chapter. Referring back to Figure 4.1 will help to recall in a simple way the purpose of all the following construction of analytical tools.

---

[1] For those who are troubled by having two different demand curves for one good, consider this: Good X, the good illustrated in Figure 4.1 has two distinction groups of consumers, each with their own unique demand curve.

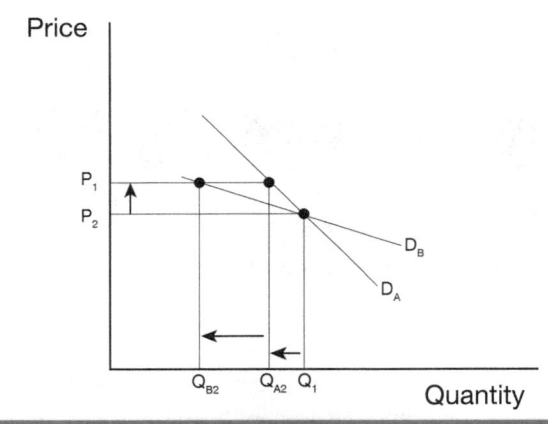

FIGURE 4.1

Definition and Classification of the Price Elasticity of Demand |e_d|

The ***price elasticity of demand***[2] is defined as the ratio of the percentage change in the quantity demanded to the percentage change in the price of the good. For some good X, the definition can be written in symbolic form:

$$e_d = \frac{\%\Delta Q_x^d}{\%\Delta P_x}$$

The elasticity of demand is a measurement of the responsiveness of quantity demanded to a price change. The price elasticity of demand is a numerical way of discerning whether buyer behavior resembles demand curve D_A or D_B in Figure 4.1.

The first property of the elasticity of demand is its sign. Perform the following thought experiment. Imagine all cars in the world are the same dark blue color. Your BFF tells you he has purchased a new car and it is dark blue. Has he shared any useful information that helps you to know what sort of car he bought? No. All cars are dark blue so no new or differing information has been shared. When an object possesses a characteristic that does not vary, it contains no useful information once the characteristic is first noted. The same point can be made about concepts; the price elasticity of demand is an example. The price elasticity is always a negative number. If the $\%\Delta P_X$ is a negative number, meaning the price of good X fell, then buyers purchase more, making $\%\Delta Q_X^D$ a positive number. The ratio of a positive number to a negative number takes the negative sign or is a negative value. Oppositely, if $\%\Delta P_X$ is a positive number, which indicates the price rose, then buyers purchase less. A smaller quantity demanded means $\%\Delta Q_X^D$ is a negative value. The ratio of a negative value to a positive value always carries the negative sign. The value of e_d is thus always a negative number. If all price elasticities must possess a

---

[2] Some authors prefer the term "own price elasticity of demand" to make explicit that the measurement is made with respect to the price of the good in question. Here it is understood that reference to the "price elasticity of demand" assumes it is being made with respect to the price of the good itself. Unless otherwise noted, references to "the elasticity" will always be references made to the price elasticity of demand.

negative value, then being told a specific good or service has an elasticity with a negative value is useless information. The negative sign is thus discarded by taking the absolute value. Formally,

$$\left| e_d \right| = \left| \frac{\%\Delta Q_x^d}{\%\Delta P_x} \right|$$

As a result of taking the absolute value of the price elasticity, the range of values for the price elasticity of demand is $(0, \infty)$.

As with most ratios, the condition under which the ratio equals one is important. For the classification of the price elasticity of demand, the number one defines the dividing line between the two categories of elasticity. If the price elasticity is greater than one, one says the demand for good X is *elastic*. Set the expression for the price elasticity of demand to be greater than one:

$$\left| e_d \right| = \left| \frac{\%\Delta Q_x^d}{\%\Delta P_x} \right| > 1, \text{ then}$$

$$\left| \%\Delta Qx \right| > \left| \%\Delta Px \right|^3$$

The inequality reads: whatever the size of the percentage change in price is, the percentage change in quantity of good X demanded is larger. If the price increases by 8%, the quantity demanded will fall by more than 8%; if price falls by 2%, the quantity demanded will increase by more than 2%. While Figure 4.1 does not contain enough information to allow for a specific calculation, elastic demand is characterized by relatively flat demand curves, like D_B. Larger values of demand elasticities reflect greater responsiveness of buyer to changes in price.

The other possibility is the ratio of the percentage change in quantity demanded of good X divided by the percentage change in the price of good X is less than one. Consider the following:

$$\left| e_d \right| = \left| \frac{\%\Delta Q_x^d}{\%\Delta P_x} \right| < 1,$$

resulting in

$$\left| \%\Delta Qx \right| < \left| \%\Delta Px \right|.$$

When the price elasticity is less than one in absolute value, demand for good X is *inelastic*. Buyers are relatively unresponsive to changes in price. The $\left| \%\Delta Q_x^D \right|$ is now smaller than $\left| \%\Delta P_x \right|$; no matter the size of the percentage price change, the percentage change in quantity demanded is smaller. When the price of good X falls by 10%, buyers will increase their purchases by something less than 10%; a 3% rises in the price leads to a less than 3% decline in quantity demanded. Insufficient information in Figure 4.1 prevents a specific calculation but relatively steep demand curves are consistent with inelastic demand, like D_A.

---

[3] Algebraically, both sides of the inequality were multiplied by $\left| (\%\Delta P_x) \right|$, which divided it out on the left hand side of the inequality. The inequality does not reverse itself or flip because it is a positive quantity owing to the absolute value signs surrounding it.

Two Alternative Methods for the Calculation of $|e_d|$

Having established guidelines for the interpretation of the price elasticity of demand, the issue of how exactly to calculate one from data presents itself. Figure 4.2 graphs the demand curve for good X. At a price of $35, buyers are unwilling to purchase any of good X. As one moves down the price axis to lower and lower prices, buyers become progressively more willing to purchase good X. For example, at a price of $25, consumers are willing to purchase 2 units while at a price of $15, willingness to purchase rises to 4 units. The demand curve is well ordered. The first method of elasticity calculation is called the **Arc Method**. To use the formula, one needs two prices and the two quantities demanded at those prices. To begin with, consider the standard way of calculating the percentage change for some variable M:

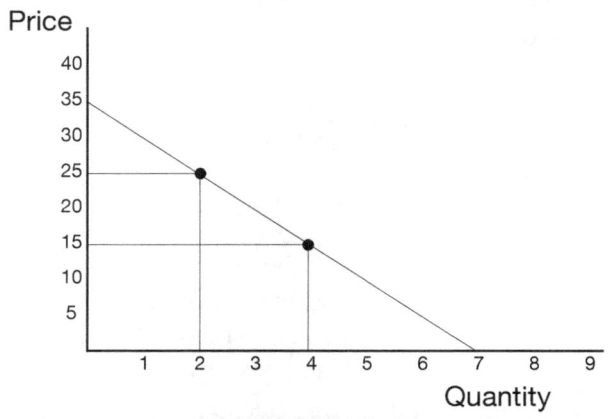

FIGURE 4.2

$$\%\Delta M = \frac{(M_2 - M_1)}{M_2}$$

In the present case, utilizing price and quantity notation and recalling the price elasticity of demand is stated in absolute value form, one gets:

$$\left| e_d \right| = \left| \frac{\frac{(Q_2 - Q_1)}{Q_2}}{\frac{(P_2 - P_1)}{P_2}} \right|$$

Starting with the price/quantity combination (2,$25) and moving down the demand curve to (4,$15), i.e., a price decrease, and then plugging into the above formula results in

$$\left| e_d \right| = \left| \frac{\frac{(4-2)}{4}}{\frac{(\$15 - \$25)}{\$15}} \right| = \left| -0.75 \right| = -0.75$$

Note the negative sign that results during the calculation when $25 is subtracted from $15, confirming e_d is a negative number. In the last step, the absolute value function is applied, rendering the quantity positive.

To verify the above result, calculating the elasticity of demand for a price increase seems prudent. Starting with (4,$15) and moving to (2,$25), then one gets

$$|e_d| = \left| \frac{\frac{(2-4)}{2}}{\frac{(\$25 - \$15)}{\$25}} \right| = \left|-2.5\right| = -2.5$$

These are significantly different answers and imply completely dissimilar interpretations about the demand for good X. In the first calculation, the price elasticity of demand, being less than one, indicates demand is inelastic. Consumers are apparently insensitive to changes in the price. The second calculation results in an estimated price elasticity is 2.5, much larger than 1. Demand must be characterized as being elastic. Consumers seemly do respond to changes in price. The difference is not because consumers are erratic. The first calculation, based on a decrease in price, uses the values of $Q_2 = 4$ and $P_2 = \$15$ in the denominator. The second calculation, based on a price increase, uses the values of $Q_2 = 2$ and $P_2 = \$25$ in the denominator. Even though the same two price/quantity data points are being considered, the use of two different sets of values to gauge the degree of change produces opposite answers for the responsiveness of demand. The first calculation leads one to believe demand looks like D_A in Figure 4.1 while the second calculation implies demand is reminiscent of D_B.

The standard method for calculating percentage change, then, produces inconsistent answers. A different method of measuring the price elasticity of demand must be adopted to eliminate the inconsistent calculations. The difficulty with the original formula stems from the different values used in the denominator depending on whether a price decrease or increase was initiated. To do away with the inconsistency, the average of the two points are inserted into the formula for the price elasticity of demand:

$$|e_d| = \left| \frac{\frac{(Q_2 - Q_1)}{(Q_2 + Q_1)}}{\frac{(P_2 - P_1)}{(P_2 + P_1)}} \right|$$

Instead of dividing by Q_2, one now divides by the average $(Q_2 + Q_1)/2$; instead of dividing by P_2, one now divides by $(P_2 + P_1)/2$. With a little bit of algebraic manipulation, one can show the 2's divide out and the final calculating formula is:

$$|e_d| = \left| \frac{(Q_2 - Q_1)}{(Q_2 + Q_1)} \middle/ \frac{(P_2 - P_1)}{(P_2 + P_1)} \right|$$

To ensure the inconsistency problem has been fixed, the price elasticity of demand is recalculated. First for a price decrease, and then a price increase. For the price decrease, from $25 to $15 and from 2 units to 4 units, one has:

$$|e_d| = \left| \frac{\frac{(4-2)}{(4+2)}}{\frac{(\$15 - \$25)}{(\$15 + \$25)}} \right| = \left|-1.32\right| = 1.32$$

Repeating the process for the price increase, from $15 to $25 and 4 units to 2 units, one has

$$|e_d| = \left| \frac{\dfrac{(2-4)}{(2+4)}}{\dfrac{(\$25-\$15)}{(\$25+\$15)}} \right| = \left|-1.32\right| = 1.32$$

The formula for the price elasticity of demand, as amended, gives consistent answers. As would be expected, the numerical answer lies between the two previous answers. Since the price elasticity of demand exceeds one, demand is characterized as being elastic although not nearly as elastic as before (1.32 vs. 2.5) and certainly not inelastic.

The alternative to the arc method of calculating the price elasticity of demand is the **Point-slope** form. One needs the value of the slope of the demand equation and one price along with the quantity demanded that is forthcoming at that price to employ the point-slope form. It is based on a more rigorous specification of percentage change definition. If one lets the differences in the quantities demanded and prices become infinitively small in the arc formula, the point-slope form results. For a demand equation of the form of $P_x = a - b \times Q_x^D$, the point-slope form of the price elasticity of demand is

$$|e_d| = \left| \frac{1}{-b} \times \frac{P_x}{Q_x^d} \right|$$

Computing the price elasticity of demand is a two- step process. Suppose the demand curve for good X is given by $P_x = 35 - 5 \times Q_x^D$. What is the value of the price elasticity of demand for good X when the price is $30? First, one must calculate the quantity demanded when the price is $30: $30 = 35 - 5 \times Q_x^D$ which equals 1 unit. Second, one inserts the values for price, quantity demanded, and the slope of the demand equation into the elasticity formula:

$$|e_d| = \left| \frac{1}{-5} \times \frac{30}{1} \right| = 6$$

Since the elasticity estimate is noticeably larger than 1, at the price of $30, demand for good X is elastic. Traveling down the demand curve, what is the price elasticity of demand when the price is much lower? Will one get the same value? Suppose the price is $5. Solving for the quantity demanded, when the price is $5 yields an answer of 6 units. Substituting the values for price, quantity demanded, and the slope into the elasticity formula results in

$$|e_d| = \left| \frac{1}{-5} \times \frac{5}{6} \right| = .167$$

The elasticity value characterizes demand for good X as being inelastic. The next section explains why such different interpretations of the demand for good X exist.

Behavior of $|e_d|$

Earlier, when the arc method of e_d calculation was used, it initially produced inconsistent answers. Calculating the elasticity of demand based on a price increase yielded a different estimate than the one based on a price decrease. The disharmony was corrected by using an average in the denominator. One might be tempted to see the difference in the point-slope elasticity estimates at different prices as also representing a shortcoming in the formula. But it is not. Rather it is a characteristic stemming from the use of linear or straight line demand curves, i.e., demand curves of the form $P_X = a - b \times Q_X^D$.

The finding of two different elasticity estimates at two different prices can be best explained by example using the demand curve from above, $P_X = 35 - 5 \times Q_X^D$. The quantity demanded at \$30 has been established as 1 unit. If the price where to fall to \$25, quantity demanded would increase to 2 units. Elasticity is based on the percentage change in price and quantity, not just the change in price and quantity. Price falling from \$30 to \$25 is a 20% decrease. As a result of the price decrease, quantity demanded expands from 1 unit to 2 units which is a 100% increase. The picture is one of a relatively small percentage decrease in price leading to a rather large percentage increase in quantity demanded. This is the essence of the notion of elastic demand.

Moving to the other end of the demand curve, a price decrease from \$10 to \$5 resulted in a change of quantity demanded from 5 units to 6. The price change, measured as a percentage change is a 50% reduction in price. The quantity demanded change, measured as a percentage change, is 20%. The picture is one of a significant percentage price reduction leading to a relatively small percentage increase in quantity demanded. The picture paints inelastic demand. Note the change in the price of good X is 5 and the change in the quantity is 1, the slope of the demand curve. The fact the changes in price and quantity demanded are the same in both circumstances results from the selection of a linear form to represent the demand curve: the slope of a linear demand curve is always the same. In the specific case discussed here, the slope of the demand curve was −5: every \$5 change in the price would produce a 1 unit change in the quantity demanded. To reiterate, the elasticity concept is based on **percentage** change rather than simply change.

The pattern of differing elasticities is consistent for all linear demand curves. At relatively high prices and small quantities, any price change will translate into a relatively small percentage change while the companion change in quantity demanded will translate into a relatively large percentage change. Thus, demand will be rated as being relatively elastic. As one moves down the demand curve to lower prices and larger quantities demanded, the price change will be become larger and large in percentage terms while the quantity demanded change will shrink to smaller and smaller percentage changes. Demand curves begin being elastic with the estimate of the elasticity exceeding 1 in absolute value. Demand becomes progressively more and more inelastic as one moves down the curve.

The last point to be made with the point-slope form of demand elasticity: the polar cases are both interesting and useful. Take the slope of the demand curve to be infinity, which is demonstrated in Figure 4.3. The consequence of infinite slope is a vertical demand curve. The quantity demanded is Q_1 when the price is P_1. It is also the size of quantity demanded when the price is significantly higher at P_2. The implication of the graph is any price, be it a high price or be it a low price, is associated with the same amount of quantity demand. If the price were to jump from P_1 to P_2, no change in the amount buyers purchase would occur. Likewise, if price were to fall from P_2 to P_1, it would cause no change in the quantity demanded. If either a price increase or a price decrease fails to alter quantity demanded, consumers are showing a complete lack of responsiveness. Computing the value of the demand elasticity when the slope is infinity, one finds:

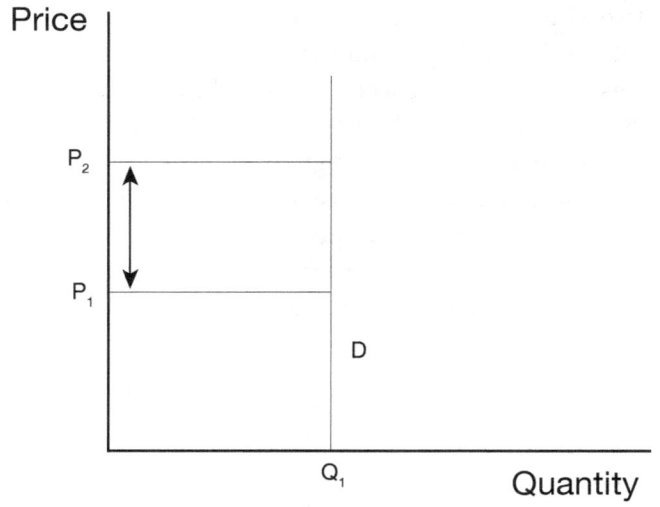

FIGURE 4.3

$$|e_d| = \left| \frac{1}{-\infty} \times \frac{P_x}{Q_x^d} \right| \to 0$$

Dividing 1 by an infinitely large number generates a value approaching zero. If the demand elasticity is less than 1, demand is termed inelastic; an elasticity measurement near zero must mark an extreme degree of unresponsiveness. When the price elasticity of demand equals zero, demand is ***perfectly inelastic***.[4]

At the other end, Figure 4.4 illustrates a demand curve with a zero slope. Such a demand curve is a horizontal line. In the graph, the demand curve is defined at a price of P_1 and buyers are purchasing Q_1 units. If the price increases, from P_1 to P_2, quantity demanded falls to zero. If the price falls, from P_1 to P_3, quantity demanded becomes infinite. These circumstances must represent the greatest responsiveness possible. Buyers can't respond beyond reducing their purchases to zero in the face of a price increase. For the point-slope formula, insert a 0 for the slope coefficient b to obtain the following:

[4] Technically, the elasticity only approaches zero but it is easier to say it equals zero.

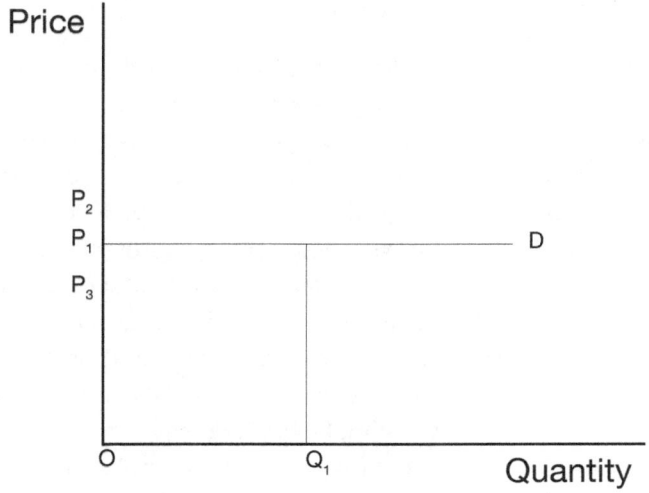

FIGURE 4.4

$$\left| e_{d} \right| = \left| \frac{1}{-0} \times \frac{P_x}{Q_x^d} \right| \to \infty$$

Division by zero is an undefined concept and is represented by infinity. Demand is termed **perfectly elastic** when the elasticity of demand equals infinity. The reader should notice the relationship between the slope of the demand curve and its price elasticity of demand. When the slope is infinity, the price elasticity is zero; when the slope is zero, the elasticity is infinity.

One last issue. A significant barrier to the understanding of elasticities stems from terminology. To begin with, if $|e_d| > 1$, demand is elastic; if $|e_d| < 1$, demand is inelastic. An elasticity of demand of 1.7 which declines to 1.3, still shows demand to be elastic. The natural way to describe the change is to say demand has become less elastic; the value is smaller. However, because changing from 1.7 to 1.3 means the elasticity measure is closer to zero, one could also say, and be equally correct, demand has become more inelastic. In either case, less elastic or more inelastic, buyers have become less sensitive to changes in price. Likewise, if the value of the elasticity moved from .56 to .79, demand is still inelastic because both values are less than 1 and the direct way of describing the change is to say demand is less inelastic. It is also acceptable and accurate to say demand has become more elastic because the value is now closer to exceeding 1.

Why Are Some Goods Elastic, Others Inelastic

Consumers show a great variation in their responsiveness to price changes. A recent estimate of the price elasticity of demand for electricity placed the value at .02, indicating demand for electricity is highly inelastic. In a different study, the estimated price elasticity for beef was, on the other hand, put at 1.42, showing reasonably elastic demand. Finally, a third study estimated the price elasticity of demand for fast food at 1.02, neither elastic or inelastic. What would explain the differences in the behavior of buyers of these various goods? Why do buyers react differently when the price of different goods and services change?

Before examining the correct reasons for the differences, a myth needs to be exercised: the possibility that any of these goods are necessities. The proper definition of a necessity is that which keeps a human alive; i.e., if it is removed, one dies and quickly. By this criteria, humans need amount to 800 to 1,000 calories and 5 oz. of water. Beyond these amounts, everything else is a want. Consider the argument that electricity is a necessity. First, very few people will expire if they are denied electricity. Second, most of the history of mankind does not include electricity. How was it possible for mankind to survive, much less evolve socially, in the absence of this supposed necessity? Why then is there a strong temptation to label electricity a necessity? Because electricity is both commonly available and has many applications. Just because an item is very useful, however, does not make it a necessity. The same type of argument can be made for cars. An automobile is very helpful: one can go from a self-determined point A to some other point B and cars are certainly common. But neither of these points makes an automobile a necessity. One should only very rarely utter the phrase "…because it is a necessity."

Number and Closeness of Substitutes

The most important determinate of the size of the price elasticity of demand is the number and the closeness of substitute goods. In the case of electricity, there are few substitutes. Nearly all appliances in the home require electricity to operate. For some appliances, e.g., water heater, stove, clothes dryer, one can use either natural gas or electricity to operate them. Of course, if one lives in an area where natural gas is unavailable, one can only choose electricity. The lack of responsiveness demonstrated by buyers when the price of electricity changes is due to an inability to switch to a different fuel. Alternatively, the significant price sensitivity for beef is easily understood. In selecting the meat to use in preparing a meal, beef is just one of several alternatives. Chicken, pork, fish constitute alternatives but they are certainly not perfect substitutes. Meatloaf is difficult to make without ground beef but one could choose to have fish tacos instead.[5]

The existence of some sort of substitute good or service will impart a greater degree of elasticity. The argument can be sharpened by considering the issue of the closeness of the substitutes to the item in question. Suppose one wants to purchase a pair of jeans. Levis jeans are a definite substitute and a close one at that, for Lee jeans or Wrangler jeans. Certainly, they are closer substitutes than beef is for pork. Likewise, a Ford is a reasonably close substitute for a Honda; again, they are closer than beef and pork. A corollary emerges from these observations. The price elasticity for a specific brand name must be larger than the price elasticity of demand for the general group. Continuing with the jean example, the elasticity of demand for Levis must be larger than the price elasticity for jeans. One can substitute all other brands of jeans for Levis as well as all other types of pants. For the general category called jeans, which contains all brand names of jeans, the substitution possibilities are limited to other types of pants. Presumably, Lee jeans are a closer substitute for

---

[5] Please do not get lost in a debate about the merits of preferring one of the dishes to the other. Focus on the point being made. Substitutes do not have to be perfect to induce elastic behavior but the closer the substitutes are, the more elastic demand will be.

Levis jeans than a pair of khakis or cargos are for a pair of jeans. The same argument can be repeated for the elasticity of demand for Ford automobiles versus the elasticity of demand for automobiles. The list of substitutes for Fords include all other brands of automobiles plus public transportation, a bicycle, walking. For automobiles in general, the list starts with public transportation, etc. A Honda is much closer to a Ford than taking a bus is to an automobile. Thus,

$$\left| e_{(Specific\ Brand)} \right| > \left| e_{(General\ Grouping)} \right|$$

Size of the Budget Share

The relative size of the item in the buyer's expenditures forms the second factor influencing buyer responsiveness. The following equation describes a buyer's annual expenditures:

$$I = (p_1 \times X_1) + (p_2 \times X_1) + \ldots + (p_N \times X_N)$$

The terms $(p_i \times X_i)$, are the price of good "i" times the annual amount of good "i" purchased and represent the annual expenditures in good "i." The equation indicates total annual income, I, is equal to the annual expenditures on good X_1, plus annual expenditures on good X_2, plus all annual expenditures on all other goods and services, up to the last one, X_N. Dividing both sides of the equation by income, I, one arrives at the budget share, si.

$$I / I = (p_1 \times X_1)/ I + (p_2 \times X_1)/ I + \ldots + (p_N \times X_N)/ I$$

$$1 = s_1 + s_2 + \ldots + s_N$$

The s_i terms represent the percentage of annual income spent on the various goods and services. The budget share for rent, s_{RENT} , is relatively large while the budget share for toothpaste, $s_{TOOTHPASTE}$, is relatively small. When one's rent increases and income is constant, the budget share for rent, which was already large, becomes larger. Likely, this will require one to make adjustments by locating less expensive housing. Whatever the specifics of the adjustment, the impact of having the largest budget share increase will lead to adjustments in the quantity consumed. Since the budget share for toothpaste is relatively small, if the price of toothpaste increases, the budget share for toothpaste will increase but it is inconsequential. Not to say buyers are happy about the price increase, it just does not require much adjustment. Hence, purchases remain essentially constant. The conclusion is big-ticket items, like shelter and transportation, which have relatively large budget shares, have relatively elastic demand. Little-ticket items, those with relatively small budget shares, have relatively inelastic demand.

Time for Adjustment

The final factor influencing the size of the price elasticity of demand is the amount of time buyers have to adjust to a price change. Consider the following story. Suppose Joe lives in a house that uses electricity to run all the major appliances as well as the small appliances. Furthermore, the major appliances are late 1980's vintage, meaning they are not very energy efficient. Joe loves the house, the neighborhood, the associated school district, etc. so he is not considering moving. Suddenly, the price of electricity jumps by 15 percent. Initially, Joe would probably consume about the same amount of electricity. It would not be prudent for Joe to sell his home immediately and move elsewhere where electricity is cheaper. Nor is it likely Joe will commence to rip out all of his old heating and cooling systems. Consumption of electricity would therefore be very similar to the amount of consumption just prior to the price hike, which is the precise idea of inelastic demand. The short run price elasticity of demand would be relatively small. Overtime, Joe might decide to add extra insulation in the attic. As the major heating and cooling systems fail, Joe would then find it advisable to replace the systems with more fuel efficient ones. The improved efficiency of the new heating and cooling systems would reduce the consumption of electricity. If one links consumption at this future point with the initial price increase, demand for electricity would be more elastic. The long run elasticity would demonstrate relatively more responsiveness compared to the short run price elasticity. In the case of electricity, the short run estimate cited above is 0.2. The same study placed the long run estimate at 0.7. Still inelastic, but considerably more elastic than the short run estimate. For many goods, there will be no difference between the short and long run elasticities. Bananas come to mind. To sum up:

$$\left|e_{(Long\ Run)}\right| \geq \left|e_{(Short\ Run)}\right|.$$

Development of the technical side of the price elasticity of demand is now complete. In the next section, several applications of the price elasticity are explored.

Applications of $|e_d|$ to Total Revenues

The price elasticity of demand proves useful when a firms needs to know what effect a price changes will have on sales and therefore total revenues. The expression for total revenues, TR, is straight forward:

$$TR = P \times Q$$

One multiples the price being charged for the firm's output by the number of units of output the firm sells. If the firm sells more than one type or version of output, then one simply multiples each different price being charged by each of the different outputs. Combining the law of demand, price and quantity demanded are inversely related, with the formula for total revenues, it is clear that changing one's price will cause quantity demanded to change and must therefore change total revenues. To increase total revenues, it is not always best to lower price.

Suppose demand for a good X is price inelasticity; that is, $|e_d| < 1$. It was established earlier than when demand is price inelastic (looks like D_A in Figure 4.1; don't forget the forest), the following holds:

$$\left|\%\Delta Q_x\right| < \left|\%\Delta P_x\right|$$

The inequality indicates whatever the size of the percentage change in the price, the percentage change in quantity will be smaller. A 6% reduction in price will up quantity demanded by something less than 6%. Symmetrically, a 6% increase in the price will lessen quantity demanded by something less than 6%. In the former case, total revenues will fall and in latter total revenues will actually rise.

Consider the demand curve $P_X = 80 - 10 \times Q_X^D$. At a price of $20, quantity demanded is 6 units. Applying the point-slope formula for the price elasticity of demand renders a value of .33[6]. Total revenues are 20×6 or $120. Since demand is strongly inelastic, total revenues should increase noticeably when the price is raised and fall when the price is lowered. Let the price increase by $5 from $20 to $25. At a price of $25, quantity demanded falls to 5.5 units so that total revenues are $137.50, a noticeable increase. If the price is lowered by $5 to $15, quantity demanded increases to 6.5 units. Total revenues equal $97.50, a significantly smaller amount. The numerical results establish a price increase when demand is inelastic causes total revenues to swell. The intuition is when buyers are insensitive to changes in price, they are insensitive in both directions. If one attempts to stimulate purchases by lowering price, little extra is sold and thus the price reduction overtakes the increase in sales. Total revenues will fall. In the example, a price decrease of $5 caused total revenues to decline by $22.50. A price increase of $5 led to a $17.50 rise in total revenues.

Consider the opposite: demand is elastic or $|e_d| > 1$. For elastic demand, the following holds:

$$\left|\%\Delta Q_x\right| > \left|\%\Delta P_x\right|$$

Buyers now show greater responsiveness to changes in the price of the good or service in question. However large or small the percentage change in the price of good X, the percentage change in the quantity demanded of good X will be larger. An 11% reduction in price spurs an increase in quantity demanded than exceeds 11%. Something more than 11% reduction in quantity demanded occurs after an 11% increase in the price of good X. As a result, total revenues rise when the price of the good or service is decreased while they shrink when the price is increased.

Returning the demand equation $P_X = 80 - 10 \times Q_X^D$, a calculation of the elasticity of demand at a price of $60 and a quantity demanded of 2 results in an elasticity of demand of 3.0[7]. Obviously, demand is quite elastic. Total revenues are $120. Suppose that price is decreased by $5 to $55. Quantity demand rises to 3.5 units and thus total revenues equals $192.50. Total revenues have increased by $72.50, a significantly greater amount. If, instead, the price had been increased by $5 to $65, quantity demanded falls to 1.5 units. Multiplying $65 by 1.5 equals $97.50 of total revenues. The price increase drove TR down by $22.50. The reasoning follows the same lines: consumers are systematically responsive. If the price is increased, sales fall dramatically, owing to great buyer responsiveness. A price decrease ignites buyer responsiveness and sales increase significantly. For elastic demand, then, the opposite conclusion results: raising price in the face of elastic demand diminishes total revenues but lower the price enhances total revenues.

Increasing or decreasing total revenues is only equivalent to increasing or decreasing profits if the firm's total costs are zero. A firm with zero total costs is difficult to imagine. However, an ability to speculate on the impact on total revenues when

---

[6] To test one's understanding, one should verify the calculations.

price is changed is helpful. Firms producing a good or service with a brand name likely face competition from other firms producing close but not perfect substitutes. Based on the arguments presented above, demand for the firm's good or service is likely to be elastic. If this is so, then the firms should know that offering buyers a carrot in the form of a price reduction causes buyers to switch away from other firms' goods or services towards their products. Alternatively, giving consumers a stick in the form of a price increase sends them off to purchase the competitors' wares.

Other Demand Elasticities

The concept of an elasticity is very adaptable. It allows for understanding not only the direction of the effect (positive or negative) but the magnitude of the effect as well. The price elasticity of demand is only one of the application in microeconomics. Elasticity measures can be constructed for any variable thought to affect the quantity demanded of good X. Two more demand elasticities are defined before leaving the topic. One for income and one for the price of related goods and services.

The *income elasticity of demand, e_I,* is the percentage change in the quantity of good X demanded divided by the percentage change income. Symbolically, one would write

$$e_I = \frac{\%\Delta Q_x^d}{\%\Delta I}$$

The income elasticity is a measurement of the responsiveness of quantity demanded to a change in the buyers' incomes. Unlike the price elastic of demand, the income elasticity is not always a negative number and hence the absolute value function is not applied. The sign, positive or negative, indicates how to classify demand for good X. Let incomes rise and thus the percentage change in income is positive. Because of the increase in incomes, demand for good X increases, indicating buyers want to purchase more of good X at each and every price. The percentage change in quantity demanded is positive. The ratio of a positive number to a positive number is, of course, a positive number. In Chapter Three, a normal good was defined as one for which demand increased when incomes rose. Thus, a positive income elasticity means good X is a normal good. Likewise, if good X is a normal good, it must have a positive income elasticity.

After an increase in incomes, it is possible that buyers wish to purchase less of some goods at each and every price. A positive percentage change in income is thus coupled with a negative percentage in quantity demanded. The ratio of the two must be negative. In Chapter Three, a good or service whose demand decreased when consumers' incomes rose was labeled an inferior good. Therefore, if the income elasticity is found to be less than zero, the good or service in question must be an inferior good. The conclusion holds in the opposite direction: an inferior good must have a negative income elasticity. Unlike the price elasticity of demand, the sign is informative: positive, a normal good; negative, an inferior good.

---

[7] Again, it is recommended to verify these calculations.

The reader should be aware that some textbooks on microeconomics make a distinction between normal goods whose income elasticity is greater than zero but less than one versus normal goods whose income elasticity measurement exceeds one. The former are termed necessity goods while the latter are labeled luxury or superior goods. This textbook finds these distinctions to be founded on imprecise thinking and does not require the reader to make these distinctions.

The calculation of an income elasticity based on the arc method calls for two data points for income and two data points for quantity demanded. For example, let income start at $700 and then it rises to $800.[8] As a result, quantity demanded increases from 30 units to 40 units. Obviously, the good is a normal good so the calculation of the income elasticity must find a positive value; otherwise, the calculation is faulty. To get consistent answers, the averaging form of the arc method is employed for the calculation:

$$e_I = \frac{(Q_2 - Q_1)}{(Q_2 + Q_1)} \bigg/ \frac{(I_2 - I_1)}{(I_2 + I_1)}$$

Substituting the specified values results in

$$e_I = \frac{(40 - 30)}{(40 + 30)} \bigg/ \frac{(\$800 - \$700)}{(\$800 + \$700)} = 2.14$$

Apparently, demand for this good is normal and purchases are quite responsive to changes in income.

The other variable of considerable significance in explaining the behavior of demand is the price of related goods. The **cross price elasticity of demand, e_{OG}**, is the percentage change in the quantity of good X demanded divided by the percentage change in the price of another good Z. Symbolically, one would write

$$e_{OG} = \frac{\%\Delta Q_x^d}{\%\Delta P_Z}$$

The cross price elasticity of demand measures the responsiveness of quantity demanded to a change in the price of some other good. The absolute value function is not used because the sign of e_{OG} will determine the nature of the relationship between good X and good Z. Suppose the price of good Z increases, causing the percentage change in P_Z to be a positive value. As a consequence, demand for good X increases making the percentage change in the quantity of good X demanded a positive value. The ratio of two positive values is a positive value. From Chapter Three, when the price of good Z increased and demand for good X rose, goods X and Z were classified as substitutes. Goods X and Z are used in place of each other. When e_{OG} is a positive number, the two goods involved must be substitutes. Likewise, if two goods are substitutes for each other, their cross price elasticity must

---

[8] It is not the purpose of this discussion to explain why or how incomes might increase. One just takes the fact that incomes have risen as a given.

be a positive number. The cross price elasticity for Budweiser beer and Miller beer should be a positive number as it should be for Coke and Pepsi.

A positive percentage change in the price of good Z linked to a negative percentage change in the quantity of good X demanded produces a negative cross price elasticity. The meaning is as the price of good Z rises, buyers want to purchase less of good X. From Chapter Three, the behavior indicates goods X and Z are complements; they are used together. Thus, a negative cross price elasticity classifies the two goods as being complements. If two goods are said to be complements, then their cross price elasticity must have a negative value. It is likely the cross price elasticity between peanut butter and jelly is a negative number.

To calculate the cross price elasticity of demand using the arc method, one forms the following:

$$e_{OG} = \frac{(Q_{X2} - Q_{X1})}{(Q_{X2} + Q_{X1})} \bigg/ \frac{(P_{z2} - P_{z1})}{(P_{z2} + P_{z1})}$$

Suppose the price of good Z rises from \$5 to \$7. At the same time, the quantity of good X demanded rises from 35 units to 45 units. The data indicate good Z and good X are substitutes. The calculation of the cross price elasticity finds

$$e_{OG} = \frac{(45 - 35)}{(45 + 35)} \bigg/ \frac{(\$7 - \$5)}{(\$7 + \$5)} = 0.75$$

Goods X an Z are therefore substitutes; they are used in an either/or way. Notice, again, in the case of the cross price elasticity the sign conveys useful information.

The development of elasticities now ends. To sum up: if demand looks like D_A in Figure 4.1, then the absolute value of the elasticity of demand is likely less than one and demand is inelastic; if demand looks like D_B in Figure 4.1, then the absolute value of the elasticity of demand is likely greater than one and demand is elastic. As will become increasingly apparent, comfort with using the concept of elasticity is needed to move on to many of the applications of economics to policy questions.

CHAPTER FIVE:

How Do People Decide What to Buy?

Future chapter to come.

NOTES

CHAPTER SIX:

How Are Outputs and Costs Generated?

Continuing to answer the question of "What can Microeconomics do for you?", this chapter looks at the internal workings of firms. In the United States economy, many different kinds of firms (or sellers or businesses, all synonymous) exist. Unlike consumers, firms differ in systematic ways and can be grouped into separate categories. The local electricity utility is unlike the local Mexican food restaurant is unlike General Motors. That said, many concepts are common to all firms. Every firm must combine resources to produce output to sell while making payments to the resources to ensure their continued participation in the process of production. This stands true no matter what their size, no matter the number of competitors, no matter how similar their products are to the competition. Three questions all societies must answer were presented in Chapter 3. The second question, "How will the items chosen by society be produced?" is addressed here by presenting production theory which makes formal the answer to the "How" question, leading directly to a discussion of cost theory.

NOTES

Production Theory

Inputs and Outputs

The basic elements of production theory are inputs and outputs. **Inputs** are any and all resources a firm uses to produce its **outputs**, the items the firm sells. Categorization of inputs enumerates four types: land and natural resources, labor, capital and entrepreneurial ability. While land and labor are self-explanatory, capital is not. In economics, capital refers to a thing, not a financial asset or transaction. Formally, **capital** is any man-made resource. An industrial strength drill press is definitely a piece of capital equipment. However, a barrel of oil, by the definition, must also be a piece of capital equipment. One would classify a pool of oil in the ground as natural resources. But to drill down to the pool, pump it out of the ground, and put it in a barrel requires a great deal of human effort. Because so much effort is necessary to arrive at a barrel of oil, it must be considered a "man-made" resource.

Outputs can be used in one of three ways. As an example of the first possibility, take bubblegum. Bubblegum falls into the group of outputs never used as an input elsewhere. It is a pure consumer good; a firm will never use bubblegum as an input in their production process. For the second possibility, consider an "e-shuttle," a machine used by VW to transport their vehicles through the painting process. A consumer would never make use of one; it is purely a capital input. An iPad makes a good example of the final possibility. An iPad can function as either a consumer good, like bubblegum, or as an input, like the "e-shuttle." Many outputs can function as inputs.

Who purchases the output fails to influence the following discussion of production and costs. Whether the output's destination happens to be consumers, firms, government or some combination of the three, the principles of production theory remain the same. Government obviously purchases some items that no one else does: nuclear weapons and tanks. But the concepts relevant to how tank manufacturers combine inputs in order to produce a tank are identical to those found in the production of bubblegum. Similarly, whether the firm produces a single output or multiple outputs, the concepts of production theory stay the same. The production process of General Motors requires much greater description than the production process of a locally owned hamburger establishment but both are regulated by the same principles.

Production Functions

Presumably, a systematic process or relationship governs the connection between the level of input usage and the level of output. The **production function** links input usage to the level of output produced. For example, the equation below indicates the output, *q*, depends on the amount of labor[1], *L*, and capital, *K*, combined by a function, *f( )*[2]:

$$q = f(L, K).$$

Table 6.1 presents synthetic production data for a hypothetical business[3]. The data in Table 6.1 adheres to the concept of a production function: the firm is producing a single output by using two inputs. The firms use labor (column 1) and capital[4] (column 2) to produce output (column 3). The labor input ranges from 1 to 18 workers while the capital input is constant at 8 units. When the firm combines five workers with 8 units of capital, 661.3 units of output are produced while combining 15 workers with 8 units of capital yields 3,153.8 units. Increasing the use of labor from 1 to 18 workers results in larger and larger amounts of output as one would suspect.

Adjustment Horizons

Firms operate in one of two dimensions of time. The **short run** is a period in which at least one input is fixed and unalterable. Some decision made about the manner of production in the past cannot be changed. Consider the local hamburger joint. The least changeable input in the production of hamburgers is the firm's location and

---

[1] Many different measures of the labor input exist: total number of hours, average number of hours per worker or simply the number of workers, the measure used here.

[2] The specific form of the function is unimportant to the discussion here. However, one common specification is the Cobb–Douglas production function which has the form $q = AL^{\alpha}K^{\beta}$.

[3] The data reflects what the firm can produce in a week. In the first row, when the firm uses one worker and 8 units of capital, the firm can produce 38.9 units per week.

[4] The analysis of production will not specify a particular piece of capital equipment like a personal computer. To investigate the productive process of an actual firm, specifics would be needed. As an aside, the Science Channel's program "How it's Made" shows how varied the productive process is across firms and industries.

TABLE 6.1

1	2	3	4	5	6	7	8	9	10	11
L	K	q	MP	FC	VC	TC	AFC	AVC	ATC	MC
0	8	0.0	n/a	$500	$0	$500	n/a	n/a	n/a	n/a
1	8	38.9	38.9	$500	$583	$1,083	$12.86	$14.99	$27.85	$14.99
2	8	131.1	92.2	$500	$1,166	$1,666	$3.81	$8.99	$12.71	$6.32
3	8	270.0	138.9	$500	$1,749	$2,249	$1.85	$6.48	$8.33	$4.20
4	8	449.0	178.9	$500	$2,332	$2,832	$1.11	$5.19	$6.31	$3.26
5	8	661.3	212.3	$500	$2,915	$3,415	$0.76	$4.41	$5.16	$2.75
6	8	900.2	239.0	$500	$3,498	$3,998	$0.56	$3.89	$4.44	$2.44
7	8	1,159.3	259.0	$500	$4,081	$4,581	$0.43	$3.52	$3.95	$2.25
8	8	1,431.7	272.4	$500	$4,664	$5,164	$0.35	$3.26	$3.61	$2.14
9	8	1,710.8	279.1	$500	$5,247	$5,747	$0.29	$3.07	$3.36	$2.089
10	8	1,990.0	279.2	$500	$5,830	$6,330	$0.25	$2.93	$3.18	$2.088
11	8	2,262.6	272.6	$500	$6,413	$6,913	$0.22	$2.83	$3.06	$2.14
12	8	2,521.9	259.3	$500	$6,996	$7,496	$0.20	$2.77	$2.97	$2.25
13	8	2,761.3	239.4	$500	$7,579	$8,079	$0.18	$2.7447	$2.93	$2.44
14	8	2,974.2	212.8	$500	$8,162	$8,662	$0.17	$2.7443	$2.91	$2.74
15	8	3,153.8	179.6	$500	$8,745	$9,245	$0.16	$2.77	$2.93	$3.25
16	8	3,293.4	139.7	$500	$9,328	$9,828	$0.152	$2.83	$2.98	$4.17
17	8	3,386.6	93.1	$500	$9,911	$10,411	$0.148	$2.93	$3.07	$6.26
18	8	3,426.5	39.9	$500	$10,494	$10,994	$0.146	$3.06	$3.21	$14.61

the size of its storefront. Presumably, the owners have signed a lease for the space for, say, 12 or 18 months, thereby fixing the inputs and making them unchangeable[5]. The period of the lease would define their short run. In the example, location and the size of the storefront are the *fixed inputs*. It is in the nature of capital goods to be difficult to alter and to be largely responsible for creating the short run. On the other hand, the labor input possesses greater flexibility. In some cases, it can be changed rapidly. For the hamburger joint to hire another busboy might take little time, perhaps one day. The amount of raw hamburger meat, the number of buns, and so on can also be altered quickly. These inputs are classified as *variable inputs*. The *long run* is a period in which all inputs are variable. Every previous decision the firm has made is up for discussion. The hamburger joint might choose not to renew its lease and move to a different location. They might decide to upgrade their ovens and grills. They might remodel the dining area. Obviously, the firm is not required to reconsider all past choices but the point is they could[6].

[5] Obviously, the firm could break its lease but this would result in expensive legal penalties.

[6] When one sees a picture of the VP's and CEO of a company standing in an open field turning spades of dirt to commemorate the opening of a new production facility, is it a scene of the short run or the long run?

In other courses and in the business media, different definitions of the short and long run are used. Typically, the short run is said to be one year or less with the long run stating at one year and extending out. How can the two sets of definition be reconciled? The economic definitions are based on a characteristic holding true; either at least one input is fixed or all inputs are alterable. The fixity of inputs must be accounted for by every firm in the world, from hamburger joints to General Motors. Likewise, all firms must also experience situations where they could reconsider all past decisions involving inputs. The rules of "one year or less" and "more than one year" are better described as rules of thumb rather than solid definitions. Many firms may in fact have lease agreements of one year or less. As location is the most fixed input, their short run would be a year or less. However, for very large firms, like Exxon, one year or less is a poor description of the length of time for which at least one of their inputs is fixed. For very small firms such as the food vendors selling from trailers, the short run is exceptionally short, possibly just a few weeks. The "one year or less" rule of thumb for the short run works in many circumstances and therefore useful. Recognize, however, a rule of thumb derives from a definition, not the other way around.

Turning back to Table 6.1, observe the column for capital contains the same value independent of how many workers are being used. The implication is the firm is operating in the short run. Apparently, at some point in the past, the firm chose a production process designed to use 8 units of capital equipment. Hence, capital is the unalterable fixed input, set at 8 units. The firm cannot incorporate more than 8 units of capital into their productive process nor can they reduce the 8 units of capital.

Marginal Productivity

The fourth column in Table 6.1, labeled **MP**, is the **marginal product of labor**: the extra output produced by an extra worker[7]. In mathematical terms,

$$MP_L = \frac{\Delta q}{\Delta L}.$$

That is, the change in output when there is a change in the number of workers[8]. To calculate the marginal product of labor, one takes the difference in successive output levels and divides by the difference in successive labor input levels. For example, when the firm uses seven workers, it can produce 1,159.3 units of output; when it uses eight workers, it can produce 1,431.7. The marginal product of the eighth worker is calculated as:

$$MP = \frac{(1,431.7 - 1,159.3)}{(8 - 7)} = 272.4.$$

---

[7] The concept and calculation of marginal product can be performed for any variable input.

[8] For the mathematically inclined, the marginal product of labor is the first derivative of the production function with respect to labor.

When the firm adds the eighth worker to the production process,[9] output rises by 272.4 units. A similar calculation shows the marginal product of the 6th worker is 239 units (900.2 − 661.3/1)[10].

Before examining Table 6.1 in greater detail, two general points need to be made. First, imagine the production process is sequential. Production begins with the first man-made resource, **K1**. The byproduct of the first process is then sent to the second piece of capital equipment, **K2**, where the next treatment occurs. The resulting intermediate form proceeds to **K3** and so on. After **K8** is applied, the production of the firm's output is complete and can be sold. Second, all 18 workers in the table are identical with respect to the components influencing a worker's productivity. All 18 have the same level and type of education, the same amount of work experience, the same level of motivation, concern for safety, and so on. Therefore, any conclusions formed from the data in Table 6.1 are *not* based on differences owing to the individual workers. The fifth worker is just as good (or bad) of an employee as the fifteenth worker.

Law of Diminishing Marginal Product

The behavior of the marginal product in Table 6.1 shows two distinct trends. At first, as additional workers are used, the marginal product rises. From worker 1 to worker 10, their respective marginal products rise from a low of 38.9 units to a maximum of 279 2. The extra output from each of the first 10 workers is getting larger. Why might this be? The effect stems from growing specialization. Since the firm uses 8 units of capital sequentially, the first worker will need to perform all eight steps to generate any output. The table demonstrates the first worker can juggle tasks and produce a modest amount of output, specifically 38.9 units. The use of a second worker increases the efficiency of production because the first worker is now responsible for only half as many tasks. He can now start to specialize; he need only be familiar with a subset of the production process. The second worker will likewise need be proficient in only a subset of the process; he will be able to practice specialization from the start. The same reasoning applies to the third work: greater specialization by the workers make production more efficient. However, the effects of specialization cannot continue forever. If they did, firms would simply grow larger and larger.

With workers 11 through 18, the second trend in the data becomes evident. Their marginal products are falling, specifically from 272.6 units to 39.9. Workers 11 to 18 certainly do allow the firm to produce more output but the extra output from each extra worker declines. The phenomenon is called the **Law of Diminishing Product**[11]: at some point the extra output produced by the use of an extra worker starts to fall[12]. As more workers are used, the contribution to greater output ultimately begins to decline. The effect owes to the short run context of production. As more workers compete for a fixed amount of capital, each worker will have less and

---

[9] Do not think "hired" but "used." Hired implies costs (wages specifically) are involved and they have not yet been introduced. At this point, the discussion is a purely technical, engineering one: how much is produced when the firm uses more labor?

[10] Technically, 238.9, which is rounded up to 239.

[11] It is also known as the Law of Diminishing Returns.

[12] The principle of diminishing product applies to any variable input.

less capital to use. It might come in the form of workers queuing up to use the equipment or maybe the capital's optimal design calls for a single worker per machine. Whatever the particulars, the extra output shrinks. An absurdly large number of workers would lead to physical crowding of the production facility, likely causing a reduction in the amount of output. If the production facility were expanded with a duplicate sequence of 8 capital units, the marginal product of the 18th worker would be undoubtedly greater than 39.2 units. The law of diminishing marginal product would not appear until a larger number of workers was reached. But since the firm is operating in the short run it cannot, by definition, add a second, duplicate production line. Conclusion: the law of diminishing marginal product is a short run phenomenon. In the long run, no single input's fixity can impinge on the productivity of any other input because no input is fixed.

Cost Theory[13]

The next set of concepts to tackle comprises cost theory. The preceding discussion explored the relationship between the inputs the firm uses and the resulting output. Now production concepts will be mapped to cost concepts. Understanding the relationship between inputs and output, while highly useful and necessary information, does not allow the firm to decide how much to produce. By mapping input usage to costs, one gains a dollar measure which can then be compared to revenues to arrive at an answer to "What level of production maximizes profits?"

Fixed, Variable, and Total Costs

In the short run, firms make use of fixed inputs and variable inputs, each of which gives rise to its own type of cost. **Fixed costs (FC)** do not vary with the amount of output the firm produces. Examples include rent on the office space or building the firm occupies or the liability insurance the firm carries. Fixed costs stem directly from the fixed inputs the firm uses. Therefore, fixed costs are only short run concept given fixed inputs don't exist in the long run. Alternatively, **Variable costs (VC)** vary directly with the level of output the firm produces. Any variable input the firm uses gives rise to a variable cost. Thus, using workers renders labor costs; using raw materials generates material costs. Since the firm uses variable inputs in both the short run and the long run, one can distinguish both short run variable costs and long run variable costs. Finally, the sum of the payments made to both fixed and variable inputs defines **Total costs (TC)**[14]. In equation form, total costs are expressed as:

$$TC = FC + VC.$$

Returning to Table 6.1, all three of these types of costs are quantified. Fixed costs, labeled **FC** and appearing in the fifth column, are $500 per week[15]. They are $500 when the firm produces 38.9 units and when the firm produces 3,426.5 units.

---

[13] Please remember profits are determined by both revenues and costs so none of the following discussion can detect the profit maximizing level of production. Patience, patience.

[14] Technically, one should call these short run total costs because fixed costs are included. Unless otherwise noted, costs are taken to be short run in duration.

[15] Remember, the data in the table are for one week's production.

Whatever the level of production happens to be, the fixed costs never change. Presume the fixed cost of $500 is the payment made to a bank for the loan the firm secured to purchase the 8 units of capital equipment. The next column in the table is the variable costs, labeled **VC**. The hypothetical firm in the example uses a single variable input, labor. The column of variable costs amounts to a column of labor costs. The assumed wage rate for each worker is $583 per week. When the firm uses one worker, who produces 38.9 units of output, variable costs are $583. When 15 workers are used, producing 3,153.8 units of output, variable costs are $8,745 (= $583 × 15). Column seven presents total costs, labeled **TC**. The values result from adding the column of fixed costs to the column of variable costs, row by row. Observe when the firm uses zero workers and produces zero output, total costs are positive and equal the fixed costs of $500. When a single worker is used, total costs are $1,083: $500 of fixed costs plus $583 of variable costs. When 15 workers are hired, total costs are $9,245 (= $500 + $8,745).

The obvious way to begin the analysis of cost theory is to think in terms of totals, e.g., total fixed costs, total variable costs, and the resulting total costs. However, casting costs on a per unit or average basis will prove more useful. The next section addresses the definition and calculation of per unit costs.

Average Costs

Production costs can also be framed as **Average Costs (AC)**: costs divided by the amount of output being produced; also referred to as per unit costs. Proceeding through the kinds of costs in the same order as above, forming the ratio of fixed costs to output defines **Average Fixed Costs (AFC)**. In equation format:

$$AFC = \frac{FC}{q}.$$

When one takes a fixed number and divides it by a progressively larger number, the ratio must fall. This is precisely the behavior observed in Table 6.1. Looking in the eighth column of the table, **AFC** is found by taking the value of fixed cost—which is always $500—and dividing by the relevant row value of output. For example, when the firm produces 38.9 units, **AFC** is calculated as $500/38.9 which equals $12.86. When output is much larger, say 3,386.6 units, the **AFC** is much smaller: $500/3,386.6 equaling $0.148 or 14.8 cents. The average fixed costs fall dramatically as output expands. Two notes: first, when output is zero and average fixed costs are undefined as division by zero is not allowed. Second, average fixed costs can never be zero. As long as fixed costs are positive, then no matter how large output becomes, average fixed costs must stay positive. They may become incredible small and close to zero but never equal to zero.

Average Variable Costs (AVC) are the variable costs divided by output. Expressed in equation form, one arrives at the following:

$$AVC = \frac{VC}{q}.$$

Figure 6.1

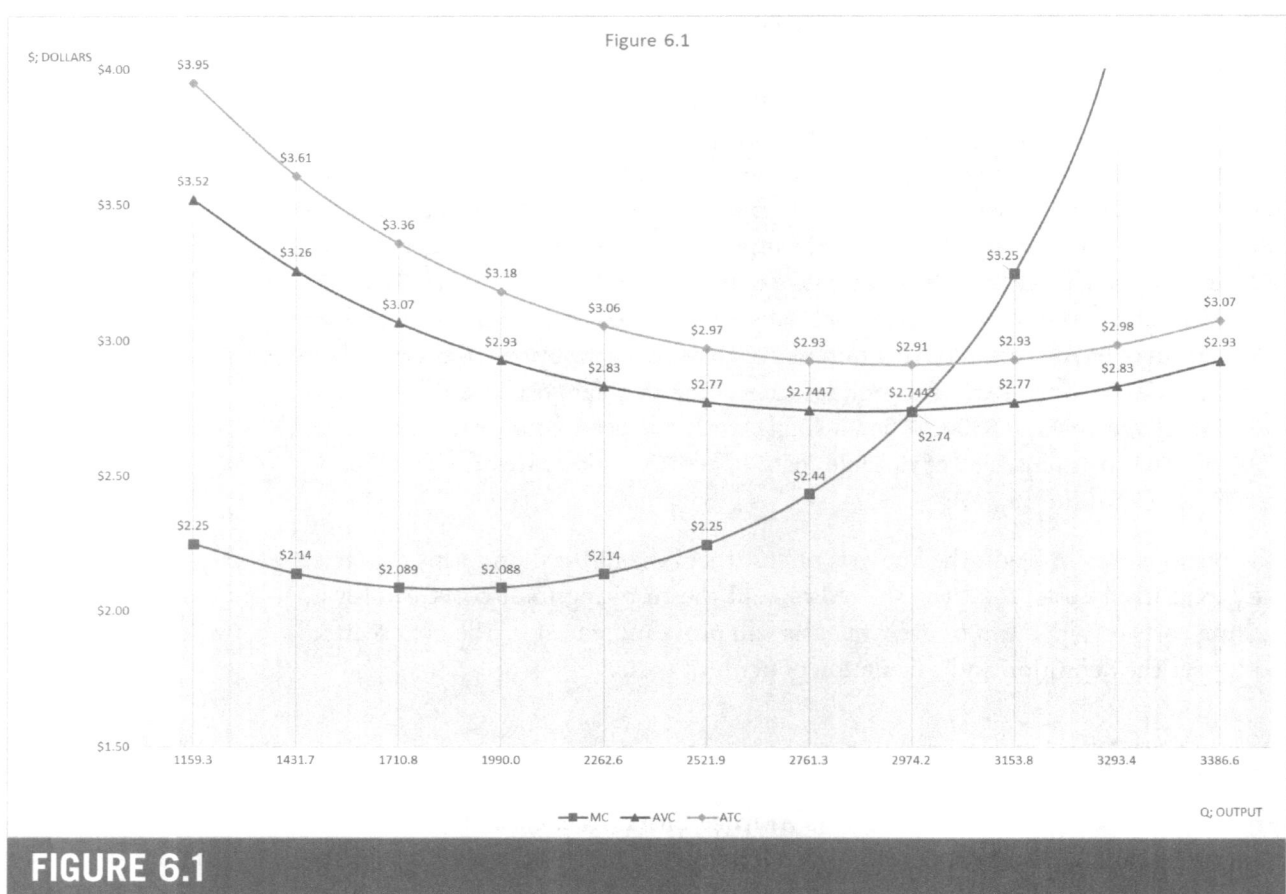

FIGURE 6.1

The approach taken to average variable costs is identical to that taken for average fixed costs: divide variable costs in a particular row by the relevant row value of output. The major difference is that the value of the variable costs changes as the level of output changes. Referring to the ninth column—labeled **AVC**—in the table, when one worker is used, variable costs are $583, output is 38.9 units, resulting an average variable cost of $14.99 (= $583/38.9). As output expands to 1,431.7, **AVC** falls to $3.26. In fact, **AVC** continues to fall until an output level of 2,974.2 is reached and **AVC** is $2.7443[16]. With the next increase in output to 3,153.8 units, average variable costs start to rise; specifically, to $2.77. They continue to rise as production levels expand. At the output level of 3,426.5, **AVC** is $3.06. The data reveal a "U" shape to the average variable cost data. It starts at $14.99, falling to a minimum of $2.7443 then rising to $3.06. Generally, average variable costs possess a "U" shape.

A useful additional to the analysis is a graphical rendition of the data.[17] Figure 6.1 plots output, *q*, on the horizontal axis versus dollars on the vertical axis. Producing output requires the use of inputs and inputs must be paid to participate in the production process, generating costs than are measured in dollars. Output is the independent variable causing costs, the dependent variable. The "U" shaped curve in Figure 6.1, marked with triangles, plots the average variable cost data calculations made in the table. The value of the average variable cost is recorded along the curve

[16] The additional decimals are needed to show **AVC** does in fact take its lowest value at an output of 2974.2.

[17] Only a limited number of output levels and their associated average costs are illustrated in the figure to aid clarity.

above the relevant quantity of output. For example, by locating the quantity 1,431.7 on the horizontal axis and moving straight up along the vertical line, one intersects the *AVC* at $3.26. The curve continues to fall to the output level 2,974.2, where average variable costs reach their minimum value of $2.7443. Then *AVC* starts to rise: $2.77, $2.83, and $2.93. The graph of average variable costs confirms the "U" shape of the average variable cost data.

Finally, ***Average Total Costs (ATC)*** are the total costs divided by output. The equation below shows there are two equivalent ways of expressing average total costs: either directly by taking total costs and dividing by output or by summing the values acquired for average fixed costs and average variable costs.

$$ATC = \frac{TC}{q} = \frac{FC + VC}{q} = \frac{VC}{q} + \frac{FC}{q} = AFC + AVC.$$

Average total costs are presented in 10th column and labeled *ATC*. Examining the first row, the total costs of producing 38.9 is $1,083 and therefore the *ATC* is $1,083/38.9 which equals $27.85. Alternatively, the sum of *AFC* ($12.86) and *AVC* ($14.99) also equals $27.85. The two calculations yield identical answers and are thus equivalent.

Returning to Figure 6.1, *ATC* values are plotted and marked with diamonds. Two features of the average total and the average variable cost curves deserve investigation. First, with the information provided by the *ATC* and *AVC* curves, one can retrieve the *AFC* data. Typically, when presented in graph form, only *ATC* and *AVC* curves are shown. Average fixed costs can still be found by subtraction. Rearranging the equation for *ATC* leads to

$$ATC - AVC = AFC.$$

The difference between the *ATC* and *AVC* must be equal to *AFC*. Looking at the graph, the vertical distance between the *ATC* and *AVC* curves is the amount of *AFC* at that output level. Considered the output level of 2,521.9 units. Extending a vertical line upwards, one finds *AVC* equals $2.77 and *ATC* equals $2.97 and thus *AFC* must equal $0.20 (= $2.97 − $2.77). Jumping back to the table, in the 15th row of the *AFC* column, the average fixed costs, calculated as $500/2,521.9 are, in fact, $0.20[18].

The second and interrelated feature to detect in both the table and the graph involves the relationship of *ATC* to *AVC*. Notice the *ATC* data also has a "U" shape. However, the difference between *ATC* and *AVC* is not constant. Since *ATC* equals the sum of *AVC* and *AFC*, its pattern must be a composite of the two underlying patterns. The "U" shape of *AVC* results in *ATC* also being "U" shaped. Applying earlier analysis, *AFC* keeps getting smaller and smaller as output expands which causes the distance between *ATC* and *AVC* to narrow. Looking back to the first row of the table, the difference between *ATC* and *AVC* is substantial: $27.85 versus $14.99, the consequence of *AFC's* large value. As output expands, *AFC* declines in value, causing *ATC* and *AVC* to grow closer. For example, when output reaches 2,521.9 units, the difference has narrowed considerably: $2.97 versus $2.77. When output reaches 3,386.6 units, the difference is even smaller: $3.07 versus $2.93. The structure of the relationship

---

[18] Check to make sure the difference between the *ATC* and *AVC* curves at different output levels are confirmed in the table.

between **ATC** and **AVC** becomes more apparent in the graph. In Figure 6.1, both curves are definitely "U" shaped. Starting at the left side of the graph, the difference is sizable. As output expands, both curves are downward sloping and becoming more similar. One then encounters the output level which causes **AVC** to reach its minimum value. Continuing along the horizontal axis, at a slightly larger output level, the minimum value for **ATC** is reached. Finally, as production expands further, the **AVC** and **ATC** becoming even more similar as the curves begin to slope upwards.

The structure of the minimum points for **AVC** and **ATC** is precise. The minimum for **ATC** must always be to the right of the minimum for the **AVC**. In the graph, **AVC** reaches it minimum point at $2.7443 when output is 2,974.2. The minimum for the **ATC** curve occurs at an output level to the right of that production level. Visually estimated, it appears to be at an output of approximately 3,064.0, which is to the right of 2,974.2. Again, though not precisely shown, the minimum of **ATC** appears to be $2.89 or $2.90. The structure demonstrated in the graph is not dependent on the data in the example. It is impossible to draw any two "U" shaped curves where the one on top is getting closer and closer to the one on the bottom as the independent variable increases without showing the minimum point of the one on top being to the right of the minimum point of the one below it[19].

Marginal Costs

Saving the best for last, the most important of all the columns in the table is the 11th and final one. Labeled **MC**, **marginal costs** are defined in equation form as

$$MC = \frac{\Delta TC}{\Delta q}.$$

The verbal interpretation of marginal costs amounts to the extra cost incurred to produce another unit of the good; the change in total costs when there is a change in production[20]. The calculation of **MC** follows a now familiar pattern. Consider the marginal cost of producing the 1431st unit. The total cost of 1,159.3 units (the previous level of output) is $4,581; the total cost of producing 1,431.7 units is $5,164. Thus

$$MC = \frac{(\$5,164 - \$4,581)}{(1,431.7 - 1,159.3)} = \$2.14.$$

A similar calculation for the 3426th unit of output shows a marginal cost of $14.61. The marginal cost curve appears in Figure 6.1 and is marked with squares.

To shed light on the pattern of marginal costs, in the table compare column 4 to column 11. As the marginal product is rising (38.9, 92.2, 138.9,…), marginal costs are falling ($14.99, $6.32, $4.20,…). When marginal product reaches it maximum value—279.2 units—marginal costs reaches its minimum value of $2.088[21]. As the

---

[19] Try drawing a counter example; it won't be possible.

[20] Note $\Delta TC / \Delta q = \Delta FC / \Delta q + \Delta VC / \Delta q$. However, since **FC** does not change when output changes, $\Delta FC / \Delta q = 0$ and marginal costs are really $MC = \Delta VC / \Delta q$ but it is easier to think in terms of changes in total costs.

[21] The extra decimal points are included to ensure the correct minimum value of **MC** is located.

law of diminishing marginal product begins to take hold and marginal product starts to fall (272.6, 259.3, 239.4,...), marginal costs start to rise: $2.14, $2.25, $2.44, and so on. The inverse relationship between marginal product and marginal costs does not depend on the specific data used in the example. It is true in general and the relationship is described by the following equation:

$$MC = w\ /\ MP.$$

The intuition behind the connection is straightforward[22]. Recall each and every worker gets paid the same amount, $583. When the firm is using workers in the range where the marginal product is rising, each additional worker contributes more additional output than the previous worker and since all workers cost the same, workers are becoming better and better "deals." The first worker costs $583 and produces an extra 38.9 units of output. Applying the above equation, one forms the ratio of $583/38.9 which gives a marginal cost of $14.98, exactly the value found in column 11 of the table. Moving to higher levels of labor usage, the 10th worker also costs $583 but produces an extra 279.2 units. Now the formula yields $583/279.2 for a marginal cost of $2.088, the same value as in the table. In the region of specialization, the expansion of output is getting larger and larger with each extra worker but the cost—the wage rate—remains constant. In this sense, each worker is a better "deal" then the previous worker and the marginal costs must be falling. Then, with the 11th worker, the law of diminishing marginal product emerges and marginal products start to decline. The 11th worker produces an extra 272.6 units of output and costs $583, leading to a marginal cost of $2.14 (= $583/272.6). Marginal costs have begun to rise. The 18th worker, who only produces an extra 39.9 units and costs $583, results in a noticeably larger marginal cost of $14.61 (= $583/39.9). These workers are becoming less and less desirable "deals," reflected in the rising marginal costs[23].

Turning to the graph, the **MC** curve is plotted along with the two average cost curves and marked with squares. Two features require further analysis. First, as the marginal cost curve is falling, both average cost curves are also falling. Next, the marginal cost curve reaches its minimum value and begins to rise. As it does so, both average cost curves flatten out. Lastly, the marginal cost curve starts to rise rapidly. The average cost curves are now also rising. The direction of the marginal cost curve seems to lead the average cost curves. This is entirely correct. Consider a similar example, much closer to home. Say one has completed their junior year of college and has a well-established GPA of 3.17. The first semester of the senior year turns out to be a difficult one, producing a GPA of 2.33. Since it is less than one's cumulative GPA, overall GPA must tumble. In final semester, a very easy one, GPA rockets to 4.00. This, of course, mean one's cumulative GPA must rise. Relating this back to costs, average costs correspond to the overall or cumulative GPA; marginal cost equate to the individual semester's GPA. Since averages are made up of one marginal event after another, it must be the case that the marginal event leads the average measure around[24].

NOTES

---

[22] The derivation of the equation is not required in order to understand the underlying intuition, but it is not a terribly difficult one. Given $MC = \Delta VC / \Delta q$, note that $\Delta VC = w \cdot \Delta L$. Substituting, $MC = w \cdot (\Delta L / \Delta q)$. Finally, observe that $(\Delta L / \Delta q)$ is the reciprocal of marginal product, $(\Delta q / \Delta L)$.

[23] A final caution: just because workers 11 to 18 are less good "deals" it is impossible to predict whether they will be hired. The profit maximizing level of production and hence the profit maximizing number of workers to hire remains to be explored in the next chapter.

[24] Identical analysis applies to batting averages in baseball or field goal percentage in basketball.

The other feature concerns the placement of the marginal cost curve relative to the average cost curves. Figure 6.1 illustrates the marginal cost curve crossing both the average variable and the average total cost curves at their minimum points. At the output level of 2,974.2, the **AVC** curve reaches its minimum value of $2.7443 which is equal to the value of **MC**. The minimum point for **ATC** was approximated earlier as occurring at 3,064 units of output and taking a value of $2.89, which is the approximate value of **MC** when output is 3,064. At the production level where **AVC** takes its minimum value, the value of **MC** at that production level is identical. The same holds true for **ATC** and **MC**. The structure of average and marginal costs is a regularity; sounding like a broken record, it is not the result of the specific numbers used in the example. The next chapter makes use of the placement of **MC** relative to **AVC** and **ATC** to locate significant outcomes in the profit maximization model.

The connection between a firm's usage of inputs and the firm's costs being made, attention can now turn, in the next chapter, to the punch line: what is the profit maximizing amount of output the firm should produce?

CHAPTER SEVEN:

What Does (Perfect) Competition Mean?

Attention moves on to profit maximization in the context of perfect competition. The first section of the chapter addresses the proper definition of profit maximization. The second part discusses the basic assumptions of perfect competition. The remainder of the chapter is devoted to locating the profit maximizing level of production and analyzing long run equilibrium.

Firms and the Goal of Profit Maximization

All private firms in all the industries pursue profit maximization. Profits are defined by the following, unsurprising equation:

$$\pi = TR - TC.$$

Profits, π, result from the difference between the revenues the firm collects and the total costs the firm accumulates. **Total revenues, (TR)**, equals the price the firm charges for its output times the amount of output produced. While **total costs (TC)** were discussed in the previous chapter, the picture remains incomplete. The following discussion remedies unfinished business.

Explicit versus Implicit Costs

In the previous chapter, two distinctions were made concerning costs. The first categorization involved the definition of costs based on the type of input considered. Fixed costs, unaffected by the amount of output the firm produces were contrasted with variable costs, directly tied to the level of output produced. Adding these together resulted in total costs. The second differentiation contrasted total costs and per unit costs. Taking fixed and variable costs respectively and dividing them by output defined average fixed costs and average variable costs; adding them together generated average total costs. The new and final division revolves around the payments made to inputs in the productive process versus the burdens borne by the owners of the firm. The payments the firm makes to the inputs listed in the production function define **explicit costs (EC)**. When a firm pays the monthly rent on the office space it occupies or makes its weekly payroll obligations, it is making an explicit payment and hence these are explicit costs. Note explicit costs can be either fixed or variable in nature. Basically, if a firm writes a check or uses some other means of payment for an item used in producing its output, it incurs an explicit cost.

NOTES

The opportunity costs the owners of the firm shoulder due to owning the business define *implicit costs (IC)*. As throughout the course, the value of the next highest valued alternative not selected quantifies the extent of the opportunity costs. For example, suppose Matt is currently working for a firm repairing air conditioning (A/C) installations. He is paid $50,000 per year by the firm[1]. Matt decides to quit his job and pursue his dream of owning an A/C repair business. In order to operate his business, Matt has forgone all other alternative uses of his time available for work. The only important alternative is the next highest valued one, presumably the job he quit. Thus, the $50,000 he is no longer earning defines his opportunity cost of operating his business. When one uses a spare bedroom to setup a home office for a consulting business, all other alternative uses of the room are forsaken. The room cannot be rented out to a tenant or used for a man-cave. Either way, a valuable alternative use of the room is given up, forming an implicit cost. The size of implicit costs can either be tied to the amount of produced output or not; thus, it can be either a variable or fixed cost.

Accounting versus Economic Profit

The distinction between explicit and implicit costs results in two alternative measures of profit. *Accounting profits* result when one subtracts all the explicit costs a firm incurs from the total amount of revenues collected by the firm. In equation form,

$$Accounting \; \pi = TR - EC.$$

Economic profits are found by subtracting both explicit and implicit costs from the revenues the firm earns. The equation is thus:

$$Economic \; \pi = TR - EC - IC,$$

$$= Accounting \; \pi - IC.$$

Both definitions of profit include all the explicit expenses of the firm. However, economic profits also include the implicit costs. As a result, economic profits can be rewritten as accounting profits minus implicit costs.

Returning to Matt's circumstances, one can illustrate the difference between the two profit measures. Suppose after opening his A/C repair business, Matt collects $100,000 in total revenues in the first year. Additional, in the first year, Matt spends $60,000 on rent for warehouse space, A/C parts, a part-time assistant, and so on. At the end of the year, Matt has an accounting profit of $40,000 (= $100,000 − $60,000). If Matt were asked how much profit he earned, his answer would surely be $40,000. To calculate Matt's economic profits, recall he quit a job which paid him $50,000 per year, which equals his implicit costs. Taking his revenues and subtracting both his explicit and implicit costs leaves a negative $10,000

---

[1] Although not part of the point being made here, do note the payment made to Matt is an explicit cost to the firm who employs him.

(= \$100,000 − \$60,000 − \$50,000). By the measure of economic profits, Matt is losing money. But at the end the year, Matt has \$40,000 in his pocket after he pays his productive inputs so how can he be losing money? Taking a slightly different view of how to interpret economic profits answers the question. Think of negative economic profits (or economic losses) not as "losing money" but as "doing worse than one's next best alternative." By running his business, Matt cannot earn the \$50,000 he was receiving by being an employee. Allocating his time to run his business results a gain of \$40,000. His next best alternative to running his business, being an employee, is an economically superior choice. He is giving up \$10,000 of earnings to run his business or he could have an additional \$10,000 being an employee. Does this mean Matt will close up shop and go back to being an employee for an A/C repair company? Not necessarily. If Matt is only motivated by the number of dollars he has left at the end of the year and is indifferent to being an employee or being an owner, then he should close up shop. Matt, however, might have strong preferences for being a businessman and is willing to sacrifice \$10,000 in earnings in order to be the boss. Two reasons why one might have strong preferences for owning a business come to mind. First, one may simply have an "entrepreneurial mindset" which renders one unhappy or unfulfilled when one is an employee[2]. Second, one sacrifices the possibility of being independently wealthy by choosing employment over business ownership. Matt will never, through employment, become a millionaire. He might, though the odds are against it, become a millionaire by running his business.

Which of the two types of profit prove more useful for analysis of behavior? Take another example. Suppose an economics professor offers the following deal to his class: if one commits to working for him all summer long, one will receive, after taxes, \$250,000. The activity does not require one to do anything illegal, immoral, or excessively dangerous. Most students would give very serious consideration to the proposal. Even if one was going to take summer school in order to graduate early, the offer should sound attractive. Offering the same opportunity to Bill Gates would receive a very different response; the proposal would not interest him in the least. The amount of the offer, \$250,000, is the same but the reaction between the two is quite different. Think of the \$250,000 as the accounting profit. The desirability of the accounting profit varies with the opportunity costs. The value of the next best alternative use of a summer's worth of time is small for the college student but large for Mr. Gates. The desirability of a certain number of dollars depends on what is being given up to acquire the dollars. Thus, economic profits, rather than accounting profits, motivate behavior: the college student agrees to the deal, Mr. Gates does not.

To summarize, positive economic profits mean the owners are doing better than any other possible use of their resources. Negative economic profits, or more naturally, economic losses, suggest the owners are doing worse than their next best alternative. The situation in which economic profits are zero defines a **_normal profit_**. When one is making a normal profit, one is doing as well as—no better, no worse—than one's next best alternative. The concept of normal profits will be explored in depth later in the chapter.

---

[2] Psychological evidence points to the existence of just such a mindset.

The Perfect Competition Model

Characteristics of Perfect Competition

The model of perfect competition is the starting point for analysis of firms. Ultimately, four different types of firms will be identified in the modern economy. The analysis starts with perfect competition because it represents the "gold standard." The desirability of the principles of free markets and the invisible hand guiding the economy to the most beneficial outcome for all of society stem directly and exclusively from the model of perfect competition. If perfect competition is not present, the desirability of free markets is degraded. For many political discussions, remembering the factors that define perfect competition allows for an enlightened discussion of the issues. Four factors or characteristics define a perfectly competitive industry:

- Many buyers and sellers, each of which is so small as to be unable to affect the market price.
- All firms produce identical output.
- Entry into the industry is free.
- The market contains perfect information.

The first requirement may be the most obvious: many buyers and sellers. It would be impossible to have much competition with a handful of sellers. However, the second part of the statement is actually more important. In perfect competition, each firm produces a very tiny fraction of total industry output. Because each firm is so small, it does not matter if the firm cuts production in half or doubles it. The international market for wheat serves as an example. There are literally millions of wheat farmer in the world. Approximately a quarter of a million are in the United States. If one of those many, many wheat farmers were to change its production decision, it would have no consequence on the overall, international price of wheat. The phrase "the perfectly competitive firm can produce as much as it wants to," which will be used throughout the chapter, may sound nonsensical. The statement is accurate because the size of each firm is miniscule compare to the total market. Certainly, if many of these infinitesimal firms started to collude, their combined actions would impact the total market. Fortunately, collusion is not a concern in perfect competition.

The second feature of perfect competition concerns product differentiation: none exists. All firms in a perfectly competitive industry produce exactly the same thing. An equivalent description would indicate every firm produces a homogenous output. In the international wheat market, wheat is wheat[3]. The implication is each firm's output is a perfect substitute for every other firm's output. The many buyers won't prefer the output of one firm to another firm. That indicates, in turn, no brand names will develop and buyers purchase output from the firm with the lowest price[4].

---

[3] Technically, five different varieties of wheat exist but within a given variety, it is all the same.

[4] The significance of the point is industries with brand names are not perfectly competitive and any conclusions reach in the chapter will not apply. Reflect on the number of items available to purchase which have no brand name. Thus, the number of possible perfectly competitive industries is reduced substantially.

The third quality speaks to the degree of easy firms can move into a perfectly competitive industry. In the market for wheat, if one wishes to become a wheat farmer, one simply acquires some land, some seeds, and a bit of capital equipment[5]. Restrictions to becoming a wheat farmer, e.g., an educational requirement or a government license, do not exist. This property will become important towards the end of the chapter.

Finally, a perfectly competitive market contains perfect information. Perfect information rules out the possibility of fooling either buyer or seller. Firms might be tempted to tell consumers of the superiority of their wheat. The consumer would reject such claims, knowing all firms produce identical wheat. Since the firms know the consumers know all wheat is the same, firms will not waste resources attempting to convince consumers otherwise.

Taken together, the four features result in a firm called a **price taker**. A price taker is a firm that exercises no control or influence over the price it receives for its output. For a perfectly competitive firm, being a price taker means the market price, P^*, is the one and only price at which output can be sold. Recall from Chapter 4, a horizontal demand curve has no slope meaning its elasticity measure is approaching infinitely; demand is perfectly elastic.

Profit Maximization: Numerical Analysis

Two alternative ways of finding the profit maximizing level of output exist, each of which will be explored in turn. Table 7.1 presents the data to be analyzed. Part of the table reproduces the information contained in Table 6.1, although not all of it. Specifically, output, total costs and average costs carry over; additional digits of accuracy are included. Three new variables and columns appear: price, total revenues, and profit. The table is based on the model of a perfectly competitive firm, meaning it is a price taker. No matter how much (or how little) the firm produces, it receives the same price for each unit it sells. In the table, the price equals $3.25. Every time the firm sells another unit of output, it gains another $3.25 in revenues. Multiplying $3.25 by the various output levels in each row reveals the amount of total revenues. For example, when output is 661.3 units, total revenues are $2,149.23 (= $3.25 × 661.3). Total revenues range from a low of zero when the firm sells 0 units to a high of $11,136.13.

Economic profits result when total costs are subtracted from total revenues, as per the equation from the previous section[6]. When the firm sells 0 units, losses are equal to the fixed costs of $500. There are no variable costs because, obviously, if the firm is producing nothing, it requires no workers. As production expands, total revenues become positive but losses grow in size. When 900.2 units are reached, losses final begin to reduce, specifically from $1,265.78 to $1,072.35. The trend in smaller and smaller losses continues until output reaches 1,990 units, which results in a profit of $137.50. Profits continue to increase until an output level of 3,153.8 units is achieved, where profits are $1,004.85. Higher amounts of production continue to show profits

---

[5] This is not to belittle wheat farming. Getting tangled up on the details of starting a wheat farm fails to advance understanding.

[6] Throughout the rest of the discussion, "losses" mean "economic losses" and "profits" mean "economic profits."

TABLE 7.1

1	2	3	4	5	6	7	8	9
q	TC	AFC	AVC	ATC	MC	P	TR	Profit
0.0	$500	n/a	n/a	n/a	n/a	$3.25	$0.00	−$500.00
3.89	$1,083	$12.8568	$14.9910	$27.8478	$14.99	$3.25	$126.43	−$956.58
131.1	$1,666	$3.8133	$8.8926	$12.7059	$6.32	$3.25	$426.08	−$1,239.93
270.0	$2,249	$1.8516	$6.4771	$8.3287	$4.20	$3.25	$877.50	−$1,371.50
449.0	$2,832	$1.1137	$5.1942	$6.3079	$3.26	$3.25	$1,459.25	−$1,372.75
661.3	$3,415	$0.7561	$4.4083	$5.1645	$2.75	$3.25	$2,149.23	−$1,265.78
900.2	$3,998	$0.5554	$3.8856	$4.4410	$2.44	$3.25	$2,925.65	−$1,072.35
1,159.3	$4,581	$0.4313	$3.5203	$3.9516	$2.25	$3.25	$3,767.73	−$813.28
1,431.7	$5,164	$0.3492	$3.2577	$3.6070	$2.14	$3.25	$4,653.06	−$510.97
1,710.8	$5,747	$0.2923	$3.0670	$3.3592	$2.09	$3.25	$5,560.10	−$186.90
1,990.0	$6,330	$0.2513	$2.9296	$3.1809	$2.09	$3.25	$6,467.50	$137.50
2,262.6	$6,913	$0.2210	$2.8344	$3.0553	$2.14	$3.25	$7,353.45	$440.45
2,521.9	$7,496	$0.1983	$2.7741	$2.9723	$2.25	$3.25	$8,196.18	$700.18
2,761.3	$8,079	$0.1811	$2.7447	$2.9258	$2.44	$3.25	$8,974.23	$895.23
2,974.2	$8,662	$0.1681	$2.7443	$2.9124	$2.74	$3.25	$9,666.15	$1,004.15
3,153.8	**$9,245**	**$0.1585**	**$2.7729**	**$2.931387**	**$3.25**	**$3.25**	**$10,249.85**	**$1,004.85**
3,293.4	$9,828	$0.1518	$2.8323	$2.9841	$4.17	$3.25	$10,703.55	$875.55
3,386.6	$10,411	$0.1476	$2.9266	$3.0742	$6.26	$3.25	$11,006.45	$595.45
3,426.5	$10,994	$0.1459	$3.0626	$3.2085	$14.61	$3.25	$11,136.13	$142.13

NOTES

but they are diminishing. Therefore, when the price the firm takes as given is $3.25, the profit maximizing level of output is 3,153.8 units and the firm earns an economic profit of $1,004.85.

While the above technique succeeds in finding the profit maximizing level of production, another approach exists; one stemming directly from the cost/benefit rule. The starting point begins with the equation for profits,

$$\pi = TR - TC = (P^* \times q) - TC(q).$$

The rewriting of the basic profit maximizing equation inserts the definition of total revenues—price times quantity—and emphases total costs depend directly on the amount being produced. Recalling a basic procedure from calculus, to find the maximum value of a function, one takes the first derivative and sets it equal to zero. In the case of the profit equation, the independent variable is q, the variable the perfectly competitive, price taking firm can choose. The level of q producing the largest profit is found by taking the derivative of π with respect to q:

$$\frac{d\pi}{dq} \rightarrow \left(\frac{dP^*}{dq} \times q\right) + \left(P^* \times \frac{dq}{dq}\right) - \frac{dTC(q)}{dq} = 0.$$

Note first the derivative of the market price P^* with respect to quantity, q, is zero by assumption: the price taker is too small for his output decision to affect the market price. Second, the derivative of q with respect to q must be one. Finally, the derivative of total costs, $TC(q)$ with respect to q, is nothing more than marginal costs. Making these substitutions, the equation becomes

$$\frac{d\pi}{dq} \rightarrow P^* - MC = 0.$$

or

$$\frac{d\pi}{dq} \rightarrow P^* = MC.$$

To achieve maximum profits, the firm should produce the level of output where the market price, P^*, is equal to the marginal cost, MC, of producing that level of output. The cost/benefit rule stated optimal decisions occur where the extra benefit of an activity is equal to the extra cost of an activity. In the current circumstance, the activity in question is how much q to produce. The extra benefit is the additional revenues the firm will collect. Established earlier, the firm receives P^* dollars for each unit it sells. In Table 7.1, the price is $3.25 so the extra benefit of producing another unit of output is $3.25. The extra cost is the amount the firm must expend to produce extra output. The information on additional costs is found in the MC column and is not a constant but depends on the level of production.

Application of the "price equals marginal cost" principle indicates the optimal level of production is where $3.25 (price) equals $3.25 (marginal cost). In Table 7.1, consider the output level of 661.3. The marginal cost of the 661.3 unit of output is $2.75 but the marginal benefit is $3.25, which makes it a desirable quantity to produce. The firm will spend $2.75 to gain $3.25. Moving to the 900.2 unit, the firm will now spend $2.44 to gain $3.25[7]. It is a wise decision to produce 900.2 units. Continuing to higher and higher levels of production, when an output level of 1990 units is reached, the firm registers a positive profit of $137.50. At the output level of 1990 units, the marginal costs are $2.09 and the price continues to be $3.25. By the $P = MC$ rule, producing the 1990th unit of output is desirable. The next level of output, 2,262.6, has a marginal cost of $2.14. It might be tempting to conclude it is an undesirable amount to produce because the marginal cost has risen from $2.09 to $2.14. A quick examination of the profit column shows profits are in fact larger at the 2,262.2 level of output: $440.45. The reason why a smaller difference between the price and the marginal costs is not harmful to profits is because they measure *extra*

---

[7] Review the section on marginal costs from Chapter 6 if the fact that marginal costs fell as output expanded does not seem correct.

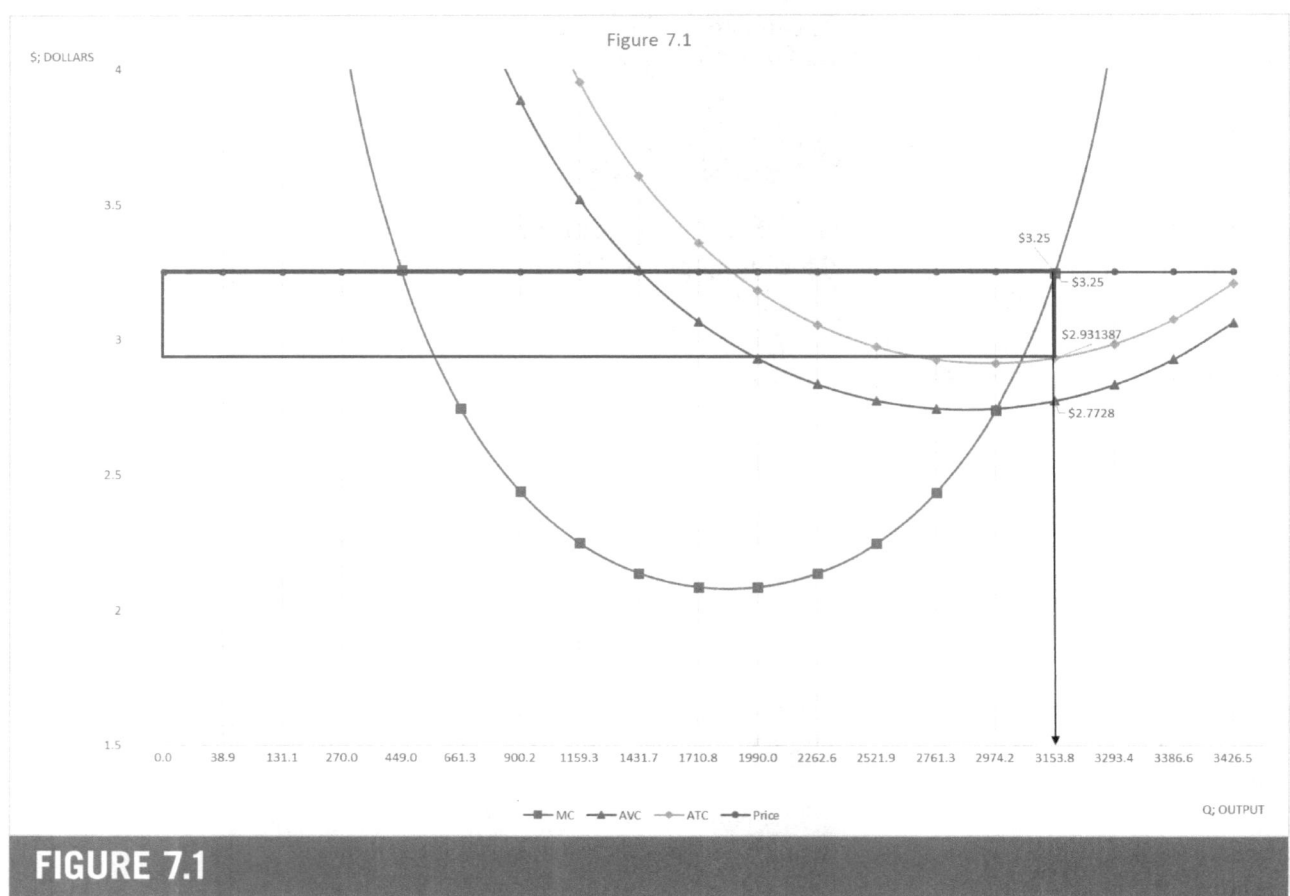

FIGURE 7.1

revenues and costs, not average revenues and costs. As long as producing an extra unit contributes at least as much to revenues as it adds to costs, then it is worthy of producing. As production arrives at 3,153.8 units, marginal costs and price are identical at $3.25. The extra revenue added by the unit just equals the extra cost. The $P = MC$ rule indicates the greatest amount of profit should occur here and it does. The firm earns $1,004.85 in profits, the largest value in the profit column[8]. Once production exceeds 3,153.8 units, marginal costs exceed price meaning the firm is producing more than the profit maximizing amount and will enjoy lower profits. Indeed, the amount of profit, while still positive, drops quickly falling all the way to $142.13 when 3,426.5 units are made.

Profit Maximization: Graphical Analysis

The analysis of the profit maximizing amount of output to produce can be extended to a graph through the use of the price equals marginal cost rule. In fact for the rest of the chapter, graphs will be used exclusively to study the material. Turning attention to Figure 7.1, one notices it looks very similar to Figure 6.1. The major difference is the average and marginal cost data for smaller amounts of output are included. Note both average cost curves are "U" shaped and the marginal cost curve still

---

[8] One might think that producing either 2,974.2 or 3,153.8 is ok since the difference in profits is only 70 cents. If the 70 cents does not really matter, the please send it to the author; he will know how to spend it.

passes through the minimum points of the average variable and average total cost curves. Additionally, the graph includes a horizontal line at $3.25, representing the market price P^*. To find the profit maximizing level of production, one applies the price equals marginal cost rule and finds the intersection of the horizontal price line and the upward sloping marginal cost curve. Dropping a line segment down from the intersect finds the optimal amount of production is 3,153.8 units, confirming the analysis above.

Figure 7.1 contains sufficient information to calculate total revenues, total costs, and therefore profits or losses. To find total revenues and total costs in the figure, recall from geometry the formula for the area of a rectangle is height times length. To calculate total revenues from the graph, one takes $3.25 (the height) and multiplies by 3,153.8 (the length) to find a value of $10,249.85. To quantify total costs, one multiples ATC by q to find TC:

$$TC = ATC \times q = \frac{TC}{q} \times q = TC.$$

Starting at the profit maximizing level of output, 3,153.8, follow the vertical line up until one reaches the ATC curve and note the dollar value, which is $2.931387. Applying the area of a rectangle formula again, one takes the ATC of $2.931387 (the height) and multiples by q of 3,153.8 (the length) to arrival at a value of $9,245. Subtracting $9,245 ($TC$) from $10,249.85 ($TR$) results in $1,004.85 ($\pi$). These are, of course, the exact values of total costs, total revenues, and profits found in Table 7.1.

An alternative way of calculating profits from the figure exists. If one takes the price, $3.25 and subtracts the average total costs, $2.931387, one finds a value of $0.318613, which is "average profit." When the firm produces 3,153.8 units, it enjoys a profit of $0.318613 on each unit. The value of $0.318613 amounts to the height of the profit rectangle. Multiplying the average profit by the quantity 3,153.8 will equal total profit: $0.318613 \times 3,153.8 = $1,004.84, which, accounting for round off error, is $1,0004.85, the maximum profit the firm earns.

The discussion so far has shown how to calculate several different measures. First, how to find total revenues for a price taker. Second, how to measure profits by subtracting total costs from total revenue and thereby find the profit maximizing output level. Third, deriving and applying the $P = MC$ rule as an alternative but equivalent method of locating the profit maximizing level of output. Finally, all the analysis and calculations found in the table can be illustrated with a graph. The next section contrasts a firm incurring a loss but which should continue operating versus a firm incurring a loss and which needs to shutdown. Detecting the supply curve of a perfectly competitive firm will then follow. Also, henceforth the analysis will drop the numerical data used above. The table will disappear; all investigation will be graphical. It cannot be stressed enough the need to grasp that the $P = MC$ rule succeeds in find the optimal amount of production and to be able to find total revenues, total costs, and profits or losses using only the graph. One should not move on with the material until one has mastered these two points.

Losses, the Shutdown Point, and the Supply Curve

Starting on optimistic footing, the firm we have been analyzing earned a profit. While it would be wonderful if the world contained only economic profit earning firms, it obviously includes many firms that are not earning an economic profit. Given that losses are a fact of life for firms, it behooves us to reason over it.

Suppose you are running a business that has earned economic profits since you open the doors 5 years ago. You then are confronted with having a quarters worth of losses. Do you close your doors and go out of business? No, of course not. Firms do not shutdown at the first experience of losses. Since most businesses begin life losing money, it follows most firms would not exist, having immediately gone out of business. At the other extreme, if you knew that, no matter what your efforts, your firm was going to lose money year in and year out for the next 3 years, would you continue to operate your business? It seems quite unlikely. Economic losses will not be endured forever. Somewhere in-between these two opposites must be the point at which the firm switches from operating with a loss and shutting down. In the analysis that follows, Table 7.2 reworks our example in Table 7.1. The columns of output, column 1, and marginal costs, column 2, carry over directly from Table 7.1. Columns 3 through 6 are new.

TABLE 7.2					
1	**2**	**3**	**4**	**5**	**6**
q	**MC**	**Price**	**Profits (Breakeven)**	**Price**	**Profits (Shutdown)**
0.0	n/a	$2.91	–$500	$2.74	–$500
38.9	$14.99	$2.91	–$970	$2.74	–$976
131.1	$6.32	$2.91	–$1,284	$2.74	–$1,307
270.0	$4.20	$2.91	–$1,463	$2.74	–$1,509
449.0	$3.26	$2.91	–$1,524	$2.74	–$1,602
661.3	$2.75	$2.91	–$1,489	$2.74	–$1,603
900.2	$2.44	$2.91	–$1,376	$2.74	–$1,531
1,159.3	$2.25	$2.91	–$1,205	$2.74	–$1,405
1,431.7	$2.14	$2.91	–$994	$2.74	–$1,241
1,710.8	$2.089	$2.91	–$764	$2.74	–$1,059
1,990.0	$2.088	$2.91	–$534	$2.74	–$877
2,262.6	$2.14	$2.91	–$323	$2.74	–$714
2,521.9	$2.25	$2.91	–$151	$2.74	–$586
2,761.3	$2.44	$2.91	–$37	$2.74	–$513
2,974.2	$2.74	$2.91	$0	$2.74	–$513
3,153.8	$3.25	$2.91	–$60	$2.74	–$604
3,293.4	$4.17	$2.91	–$236	$2.74	–$804
3,386.6	$6.26	$2.91	–$548	$2.74	–$1,132
3,426.5	$14.61	$2.91	–$1,015	$2.74	–$1,605

Breakeven Operation Using the Numbers

Table 7.2, column 4, shows the profit status of the firm when the price falls to $2.91. Before we consider the column of profits, the level of production needs to be located. Recall the Cost/Benefit Principle says continue taking an action as long as the extra benefit exceeds or is equal the extra cost. The extra benefit of selling an extra unit is $2.91 when the price is $2.91. Examining the marginal cost in column 2, there is no level of production that causes $2.91 worth of extra cost. One must therefore pick the value of marginal cost closest to $2.91 without exceeding it. This would be an output level of 2,974.2 units where the marginal cost is $2.74. Moving over to the column of profits, we see two points. One, when the firm produces 2,974.2 units it has zero economic profits, i.e., it is at the breakeven price. Two, confirming the Cost/Benefit Principle, any other level of production results in losses. For example, production of the amount that maximized profits when the price was $3.25, 3,923 units, now causes $236 worth of losses. Likewise, producing the amount 2,761.3 results in a negative profit of $37. Neither of these are as welcome as breaking even. To sum up, when the price is $2.91, the firm's best choice is to produce 2,974 units and breakeven.

The Shutdown Point

Firms will not continue to operate regardless of the impact on economic profits. Consider what happens if the price falls to $2.74. We know that if a price of $2.91 causes zero profits, then anything less than that will cause economic losses. So, indeed, by looking in the column 6 in Table 7.2, where profits when the price is $2.74 are calculated, every element is negative. But something more is going on as well. Note the smallest amount of loss in column 6 when production is positive is $513. If the firm chooses not to operate, to be shutdown, it will still have to pay its fixed costs. Those fixed costs are only $500. Which means it is better for the firm to close its doors than to remain open.

The following rules state the relationship between revenues, variable costs and the decision to remain operating.

$$\text{If } TR \geq VC, \quad \text{operate}$$
$$\text{If } TR < VC, \quad \text{shutdown}$$

The condition says if the firm cannot pay all of its variable costs, then it should shutdown. Think about the following example. Suppose you were to go to work and on payday your boss says he can't pay you because he does not have the revenue to do so. You will react poorly. You likely will not return to work except to demand the back pay you are owed. And since you are not at work, the business cannot produce as much as it was, thus lowering it revenues even more. With less revenue, the boss can afford to pay even fewer worker and they quit. This highlights the impossibility of a firm operating if it can't pay, at a minimum, its variable costs.

The rule stated above and also be expressed using average costs. First divide both sides of the inequality by q.

$$\text{if} \quad \frac{TR}{q} \geq \frac{VC}{q}$$

$$\text{then} \quad P \geq AVC$$

Then recognize that VC divided by q is average variable costs and TR divided by q is price. As long as the price the firm receives is greater than its average variable cost, it should continue to operate. If the price the firm is getting is less than AVC, then the firm should shutdown. This interpretation of the shutdown condition allows for a graphical depiction.

The Shutdown Point Using the Graph

Turning now to graphical analysis, Figure 7.2 illustrates the a firm's cost curves: AVC, ATC, and MC. Quickly, let us recall a few facts about these 3 curve. (1) As output reaches larger and larger levels, the AVC and ATC curves get closer to on another; (2) both AVC and ATC are "U"-shaped which means let both have minimum points and the minimum point for ATC is to the right of the minimum point on AVC and (3) the MC curve runs through the minimum points of AVC and ATC[9].

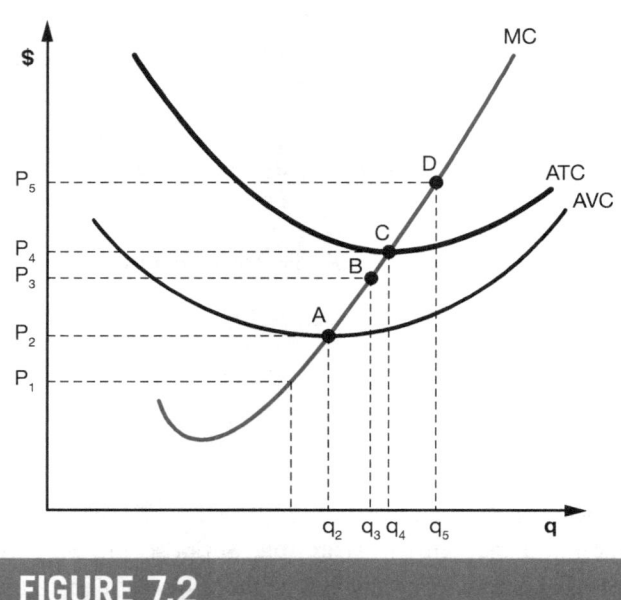

FIGURE 7.2

Five different prices are illustrated in Figure 7.2. The first price, P_1, is an example of a price that would cause the firm to shutdown. It is below the AVC curve so price is less than average variable costs. In fact any price below P_2 will cause the firm to shut its doors. The first price that allows for the firm to operate is P_2. Since P_2 intersects the

---

[9] If the three points sound unfamiliar or confusing to you, please review the material in the second half of Chapter 6.

AVC curve at its minimum point, $P = AVC$, which is the first point firms can cover their variable costs. Hence they are able to operate. How much should they produce? Follow the $P = MC$ rule. The fact that MC runs through the same minimum point tells us the profit maximizing level of output is found by dropping straight down to the q axis and marking q_2. This point is marked as "A" in the graph. The next price mark on the vertical axis is P_3. At this price the firm is operating because price is above AVC. Applying the $P = MC$ rule, the proper amount of output is q_3.This point is marked as "B." The firm is, however, earning a loss because P_3 is always below the ATC curve. The fourth price, P_4, runs through the minimum point of ATC which means $P = ATC$. The optimal amount to produce is q_4 by the $P = MC$ rule and is marked by point "C." Obviously, if the firm will operate at prices P_2 and P_3, it will operate at a still higher price. The important fact to remember about P_4 is total revenues and total costs are the same, hence the firm is breaking even. That is, profits are zero. Finally, P_5 is the highest price of all and the $P = MC$ rule shows that q_5 is the profit maximizing level of output and is marked by point "D." The firm is now earning a profit because $P > ATC$ which means $TR > TC$.

Notice how, in the graph, higher prices (P_2, P_3, P_4, & P_5) means greater output (q_2, q_3, q_4, & q_5). In other words, as firms pursue profit maximization, higher prices means greater output while lower prices means lesser output. This is the essence of the concept of supply. The firm's supply curve starts at point "A" and continues up to "B" then "C" and then "D" and beyond.

The Industry Supply Curve

Deriving the industry supply curve requires we horizontally sum the individual firms' supply curves. Consider the situation depicted in Figure 7.3. There are graphs of two firms, Firm A & firm B and one labeled the Market and they are arranged side by side by side. The graphs of the firms contain their marginal cost curves. For Firm A, the shutdown price is P_{SD}^A so the portion of the MC illustrated is its supply curve. They produce 2 units at their shutdown price. Firm B has a higher shutdown price at P_{SD}^B. They produce 7 units at their shutdown price. The graph also shows that Firm A is producing 4 units at Firm B's shutdown price, P_{SD}^B. The market supply curve is found by simply adding the two MC curves at each different price.

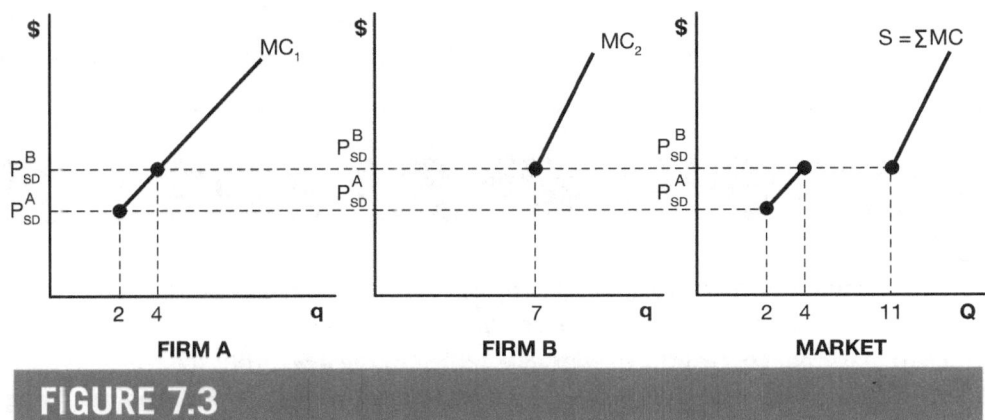

FIGURE 7.3

Therefore, the market supply does not exist at prices below P_{SD}^A. From P_{SD}^A to P_{SD}^B, the market supply curve is equal to Firm A's and starts at 2 and increases to 4 units. Then at P_{SD}^B Firm B begins to operate and produces the 7 units. This shifts the market supply curve to right to 11 units. Four of them come Firm A and 7 come from Firm B. As price continues to rise, the market supply is the addition or horizontal summation of the 2 *MC* curves.

In a perfectly competitive market there are many firms, many more than 2. But the idea is the same: note how much each firm produces at each different price, add them together and trace out the market supply curve.

The Long Run

The third assumption of perfect competition is the firm has the freedom to enter or exit the market anytime they want. There are no barriers to entry. This is the key to understanding the long run in perfect competition.

Looking at Figure 7.4, one sees a market in competitive equilibrium. On the left-hand side is the market where market supply and market demand intersect, determining an equilibrium price of P_0. On the right hand side is one of the many, many small firms. The equilibrium price is the price the firm takes as given, i.e., they use the price P_0 to determine the profit maximizing output. The proper amount to produce is found by applying the profit maximizing rule of $P = MC$ and is marked q_0. Notice also the firm is earning zero economic profits at that point. Recall this means the firm is doing as well as its next best alternative. Therefore, the owners of the firm will continue to stay in the industry.

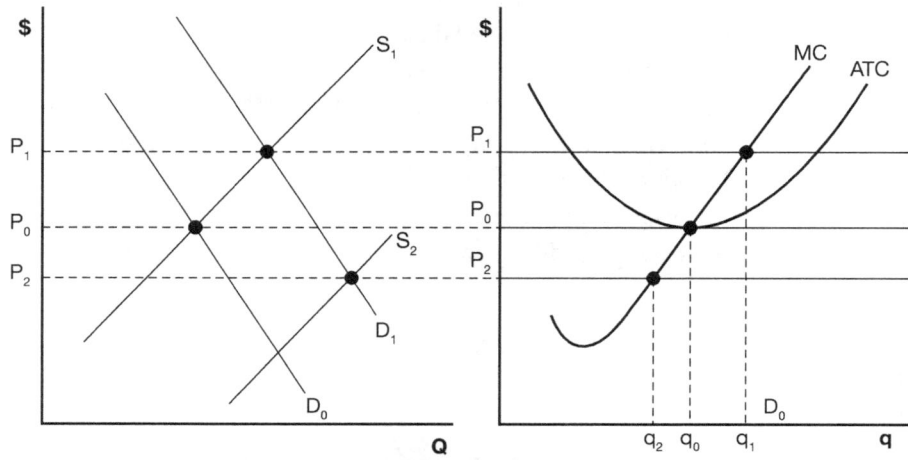

FIGURE 7.4

Now assume consumers' income increases, shifting demand from D_0 to D_1. As a result, price rises to P_1. The firm now reevaluates it production decision. Equating price to marginal costs at the new price establishes the new profit maximizing output q_1. The important consequence of the price increase is the firm is now earning an economic profit, meaning they are doing better than their next best alternative.

The economic profits serve as an incentive for new firms to join the industry. Clearly, at any point in time firms in other closely related industries are not earning economic profits. They will shift to producing the good for which firms are earning economic profits. Moreover, brand new firms will be formed to produce the good. Remember the industry supply curve is the sum of all the individual marginal cost curves so the entry causes the supply curve to shift from S_1 to S_2. The supply shift is large enough to drive the equilibrium price down to P_2. Now the equilibrium price is below the break-even price which must mean firms are earning economic losses. Firms are doing worse than their next best alternative. This leads to firms exiting the industry. While not illustrated in Figure 7.4, this exit will cause the supply to shift to the left because there are now fewer firms in the industry. The leftward shift causes the equilibrium price to rise, leading to some degree of economic profits and therefore entry by new firms. The cycle is now complete. First, we have economic profits which leads to new firm joining the industry. Then we have economic losses leading to firm exiting the industry. This leads to a new round of economic profits, entry of new firms, then economic losses, exit of firms and so on. The process only stops when zero economic profits are reestablished. The number of firms becomes stable.

This concludes our discussion of perfect competition. Next we examine the polar opposite of perfect competition: monopoly.

CHAPTER EIGHT:

What Does Monopoly Mean?

The second type of market structure is monopoly. It is the direct opposite of perfect competition.

The Assumptions of the Monopoly Model

Just as in perfect competition, assumptions or characteristics of a monopoly market need to be enumerated. They are:

- A single firm
- No close substitutes
- Barriers to entry

The first assumption is obvious; there is only one firm in a monopoly market. "Mono" is Latin for one. However, we should recognize that all firms who produce branded products are single firms. Levi's is the only company that can produce Levi's jeans; Anheuser Busch is the only company that can produce Budweiser beer. Branded product can only be sold by the company holding the trademark. But no one would argue Levi's is the monopoly supplier of jeans because there are many good substitutes for Levi's jeans: Lee or Wrangler. This is not the case for monopoly for there are no close substitutes. As discussed in Chapter 4, electricity is a good that has no close substitutes and it is sold by monopolies. Finally, there are either economic or legal barriers to entry. No one can simple set up a competing firm in a monopoly market.

Taken together this means a monopolist is a *price-maker*: he faces the entire, downward sloping market demand curve rather than a very small piece of the market as in the case of a perfectly competitive firm.

Total and Marginal Revenue

The relationship between revenues and additional sales is different for monopoly than it is for perfect competition. First, let us define marginal revenue (**MR**) as the extra revenue the firm gains from the sale of extra unit of output. Formally,

$$MR = \frac{\Delta TR}{\Delta q}.$$

The contrast between **MR** to a perfectly competitive firm and **MR** to a monopolist is illustrated in Figure 8.1. On the left hand side is a perfectly competitive while on the right side is a monopolist. To start both firms are selling at a price of $5 with a quantity of 100 units. This means both firms are collecting $500 in total revenues (**TR**). When the perfectly competitive firm sells an additional unit, **TR** rises to $505 ($5 × 101). The **MR** is ($505 − $500)/(101 − 100) which equals $5, the price at which the perfectly competitive firm sells its output. In the case of perfect competition, price and marginal revenue are equal. As shown in the graph, the perfect competitor experiences only a gain in revenues when he sells another unit.

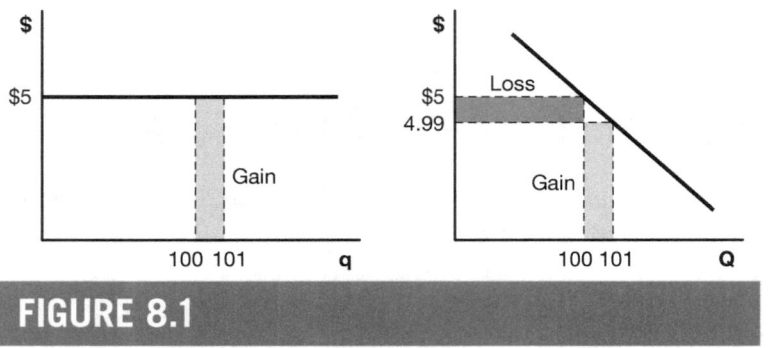

FIGURE 8.1

Matters are different for the monopolist. He likewise sells 100 units for $5 a piece meaning his **TR** is $500. However, to sell one more unit, the monopolist must lower his price. In the example he must lower his price to $4.99. His **TR** is now $503.99 ($4.99 × 101). Calculating the monopolist's **MR**, one finds it is $3.99 ($503.99 − $500.)/(101 − 100), which is less than the price he is charging. This is because, as illustrated in the graph, the monopolist has an area of gain, where he sells one more unit for $4.99. But he also has an area of lost revenues because he had to lower the price to $4.99 on the first 100 units. Multiplying one penny times 100 units equals $1. Subtracting the loss from the gain ($4.99 − $1.00) one gets the marginal revenue figure of $3.99.

It is always the case that for a monopolist, the marginal revenue of a sale will be less than the price being charged. This point can be made with a general mathematical setup. First, the monopolist's demand curve is.

$$P = a - bQ.$$

This mean **TR** becomes

$$TR = P * Q$$

$$TR = (a - bQ) * Q$$

$$TR = aQ - bQ^2.$$

Taking the derivative of **TR** with respect to **Q** leads to

$$MR = \frac{dTR}{dQ} = a - 2bQ.$$

If we compare the slope coefficient for the demand curve (−**b**) to the marginal revenue curve (−**2b**), we see the slope of **MR** is twice as steep as the demand curve.

A numerical example is in order. If the demand curve is

$$P = 10 - 5Q$$

then the **MR** curve is

$$MR = 10 - 10Q$$

Figure 8.2 provides a graph of both the demand curve and the marginal revenue curve. Notice how the **MR** curve is always below the demand curve. If we consider a specific output level, say **Q′**, and draw a straight line up to the demand curve , we see the price is **P′** while the marginal revenue is less at **MR′**.

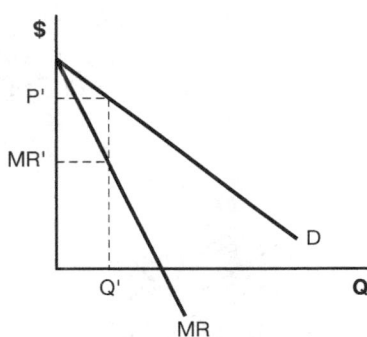

FIGURE 8.2

Profit Maximization: Graphical Analysis

In the last chapter, we found the profit maximizing condition for the perfectly competitive firm was to produce where price equals marginal cost. That rule will not work for the monopolist because price and **MR** are not the same value. Consider the following equation of profits

$$\pi = TR(Q) - TC(Q).$$

Both total revenues and total costs depend on output so we can take the derivative with respect to **Q** as

$$\frac{d\pi}{dQ} \rightarrow \frac{dTR}{dQ} - \frac{dTC}{dQ} = 0$$

which can be re-expressed in more familiar notation as

$$\frac{\Delta TR}{\Delta Q} - \frac{\Delta TC}{\Delta Q} = 0$$

or finally as

$$MR = MC.$$

The rule indicates the best possible output to produce is the one where marginal revenues equal marginal cost. This is the general form of the profit maximizing rule and it always applies to every firm. In perfect competition, $P = MR$ so one can either express the condition as either $P = MC$ or $MR = MC$. But for monopolists, the only correct statement is $MR = MC$.

In Figure 8.3, we see a monopolist making a profit maximizing output decision. The point at which $MR = MC$ is marked as A. To find the output level that maximizes profit drop a straight line down from point A to the horizontal axis. This point is marked Q^*, the profit maximizing level of output. Our work is not finished, however. We must determine the price the monopolist is going to charge for his output. This information is found on the demand curve. Bounce up from Q^* until we hit the demand curve at point B, then take a straight line across to the vertical axis. The price is marked as P^*. The profit maximizing point for the monopolist is to produce Q^* and charge a price of P^*.

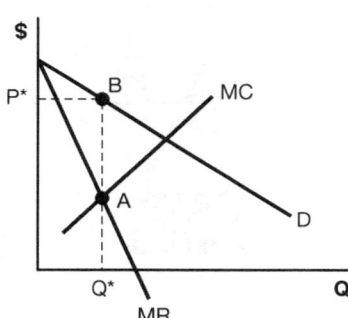

FIGURE 8.3

In the next section, we consider how the presence of monopolies harm the economy.

The Social Harm of Monopoly

If one were to casually ask someone whether monopolies were good or bad they would undoubtable answer they are harmful to the economy. What we need to understand is the correct reason for this conclusion.

Monopolies Can Charge Any Price They Choose

No firm has the ability to charge any price they wish. Demand curves are downward sloping and the monopolist can not violate the negative relationship between price and quantity demanded. Going back to Figure 8.3, the most the monopolist can charge for the output level Q^* is P^*. If they try to charge any price higher than P^* they will sell an amount less than Q^*.

Monopolies Always Earn Large Economic Profits

Monopolies are not guaranteed to earn accounting profits much less economic profits. Figure 8.4 shows how easy it is to illustrate a monopolist making a loss. The main issue is that being a monopolist does not mean that the costs of production are low. From the argument made above, we know the monopolist cannot simply pass along it costs to consumers in the form of a higher price, It is, however, true that if a monopolist is earning positive economic profits, the barriers to entry means no competitors will enter the market and drive profits to zero as is the case in perfect competition.

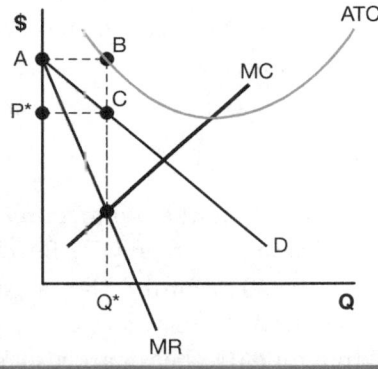

FIGURE 8.4

Monopolies Always Underproduce and Overcharge

The correct reason for saying monopolies are harmful to the economy rests with the fact that they always produce less and charge more than the social optimal amount. Figure 8.5 displays a monopolist making a profit maximizing decision. He has located the point at which $MR = MC$ and is producing Q^* charging a price of P^*. Now let's assume that the monopolist's MC curve is the supply curve that would emerge if the market was converted to perfectly competition, i.e., $MC = S$. Now the equilibrium is just like the equilibrium from Chapter 3: where supply intersects demand. The resulting quantity is Q' and the price is P'. The perfectly competitive outcome is considered the socially optimal one. The monopolist is charging a price higher than the best value and producing less than the optimal amount. This means economic activity is smaller than it could be.

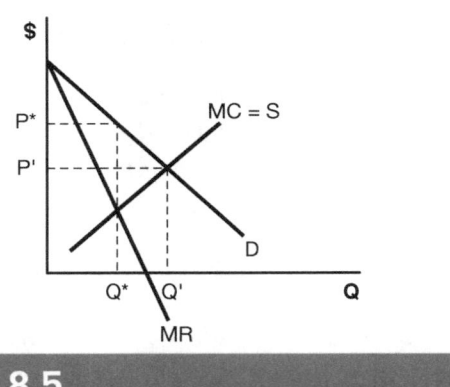

FIGURE 8.5

Sources of Market Power

Now that the model of monopoly is complete, we can turn to factors that give rise to a firm having **market power**. Market power is simply defined as a firm that can raise its price without losing all of its sales. Perfectly competitive firms have no market power because if they raise their price above the market price, consumers will all shift to another perfectly competitive firm. Any firm that faces a downward sloping demand curve has some degree of market power.

Control of an Important Input

If a firm controls an input important to the production process, it will enjoy some degree of market power. The diamond company De Beers had an effective monopoly in the diamond market in the 20th century. They accomplished this by systematically acquiring as many diamond mines as they could, effectively controlling the market for raw diamonds. In the 1980's, their market share of rough diamonds was as high as 90%. This gave them significant market power.

Patents

The process of a patent works as follows. A claim is made and is considered patentable if it is useful, novel or non-obvious. This ensure that in most cases a close substitute will not exist, meeting one of the characteristic of monopoly. If the patent is granted, the inventor will have exclusive ownership of the patent for 20 years. In order words, he will be the sole supplier of the item for which there are barriers to entry, thus fulfilling the other two characteristics of monopoly.

Why would taxpayers want the government to grant monopolies since we know monopolies produce less economic output? The answer is to protect the incentive for firms to engage in research and development. If there were no patent law, when a firm developed a new product and introduced it to the marketplace, other firms would merely reverse engineer it and sell their own version without having to bear the development costs.

Economies of Scale

In the long run, both labor and capital are variable. This leads to an interesting question: If the amount of inputs being used is doubled, what happens to output? If output exactly doubles, this is called **constant returns to scale**. If output more than doubles, it is termed **increasing returns to scale**. **Decreasing return to scale** occur when output less than doubles. For example, the firm could be using 10 units of labor, 5 units of capital and producing 70 units of output. If those inputs are doubled to 20 units of labor and 10 units of capital, output could rise to 150 units. Since this is more than a doubling of output, the firm is experiencing increasing returns to scale.

Next, let us assume the 10 units of labor cost $50 and the 5 units of capital cost $100, giving us total costs of $150. When input usage doubles, total costs also double to $300 because we are using twice as much labor and capital. Notice what happens to average total cost: they fall from $2.14 ($150/70) to $2 ($300/150). When average total costs fall as output expands, the firm is said to be experiencing **economies of scale**. It is the cost side counterpoint to increasing returns to scale.

In some industries economies of scale exist over nearly all output level. Electricity is an example. The larger the generator, the lower the average costs. In these circumstances, one firm will emerge to supply the entire market. A single firm that results due to extended economies of scale is called a **natural monopoly**.

Network Economies

Network economies are said to exist when the usefulness of a good depends on the number of consumers using the good. The first fax machine was of little value until a second one was in service. A more current example occurred between the video tape standards of VHS and Sony's Betamax ("Beta"). Beta had a superior picture quality but could initially only record an hour's worth of programming while VHS could record up to six hours' worth of programs. Consumers preferred the longer record times. By the time Sony expanded Beta's record time, it was too late. Video rental stores were stocking VHS tapes nearly exclusively. Consumer trying to decide which standard to purchase had a strong incentive to select VHS, which in turn reinforced the rental store's tendency to acquire only VHS versions of movies, thus reinforcing new consumers to select VHS, etc. Soon Beta had disappeared from the market. A similar phenomena played out in the competition between Blu-Ray and HD DVD. This time the Sony product won out.

Price Discrimination

The final topic for monopoly is **price discrimination**. Price discrimination is the situation where a firm charges different prices to different consumers even though the marginal cost of production is the same. Examples abound: different prices for movie tickets depending on one's age; differential pricing for flying during the week rather than the weekend; senior discounts at Luby's and Golden Corral.

CHAPTER NINE:

Monopolistic Competition and Oligopoly

Monopolistic competition and oligopoly fall between the two extremes of perfect competition and monopoly, having some of the characteristics of both.

Assumptions of Monopolistic Competition

1. Buyers and sellers are numerous
2. Firms produce a slightly differentiated product
3. Ease of entry

Monopolistic competition is closer to perfect competition than monopoly in the sense that monopolistic competition also has many sellers and ease of entry. These assumptions will mean, in the long run, that monopolistic competition like perfect competition will make only a normal profit. Monopolistic competition is closer to monopoly in the sense that they produce a differentiated product. This is what gives a monopolistically competitive firm some pricing power, the ability to raise price and still sell something. The closest business to monopolistic competition is fast food. There are many places to get a burger. They all produce burgers, however, they are not exactly the same. A McDonald's burger is different from a burger at Burger King. There is ease of entry in the burger industry. If McDonald's makes more money selling Big Macs than Burger King's Whopper makes, Burger King could produce a similar burger—the Big King. They use the same equipment to make the Big King as they did for the Whopper so it is very easy to compete away any excessive economic profits at McDonald's.

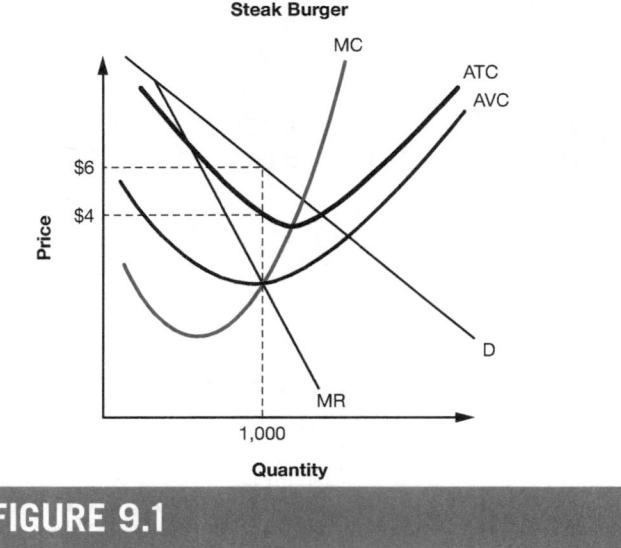

FIGURE 9.1

Refer to the graph above. The first restaurant to make a steak burger was Steak 'n Shake. To calculate their economic profits in the short run use the following formula.

$$\text{Profit} = (P - ATC)Q$$

Remember the order of operations! Do parentheses first then multiply. The first thing you always want to find is quantity (Q). Remember the goal of all businesses is to maximize profits. All firms maximize profits by producing where MR = MC. The profit maximizing quantity is 1,000. Once you have found quantity go up to what you want. To find price go up from 1,000 to the demand curve. The price is $6. Then find the ATC. To find the ATC go from 1,000 to the ATC curve. The ATC is $4.

Their economic profit in the short run would be:

$$\text{Profit} = (6 - 4)1,000 = \$2,000 \text{ economic profit.}$$

So, in the short run, Steak 'n Shake makes more money than the other burger places. A positive economic profit is a signal to enter. In the long run other burger places will want to enter and compete away any economic profits. One of the assumptions of monopolistic competition is ease of entry. Other burger places will start making steak burgers. They will use the same grills and employees that they had made hamburger to now make steak burgers as well. So it is very easy to enter in and compete. To get customers to try their product they must offer a lower price than Steak 'n Shake. Steak burgers from Steak 'n Shake and other burger places are substitute goods. So, by entering into the steak burger market, other burger places are lowering the price of a substitute. Whenever you lower the price of a substitute demand will decrease (shift to the left).

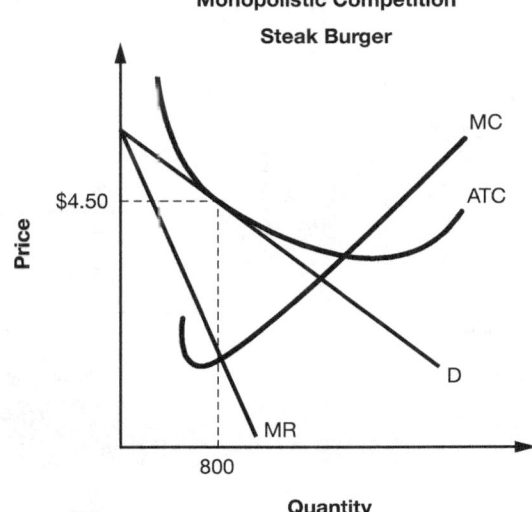

Monopolistic Competition

Steak Burger

FIGURE 9.2

Refer to the graph above. In the long run a monopolistically competitive firm will produce 800 steak burgers at a price of $4.50 each. To calculate the firm's economic profit in the long run use the profit formula:

$$\text{Profit} = (P - ATC)Q$$

The first thing you always want to find is quantity (Q). Remember the goal of all businesses is to maximize profits. All firms maximize profits by producing where MR = MC. The profit maximizing quantity is now 800. Once you have found quantity go up to what you want. To find price go up from 800 to the demand curve. The price is $4.50. Then find the ATC. To find the ATC go from 800 to the ATC curve. The ATC is $4.50. Remember the order of operations! Do parentheses first then multiply.

Refer to the graph above. Profit = (4.5 − 4.5) 800 = $0 economic profit. In the long run equilibrium for a monopolistically competitive firm their demand is just tangent (touching at one point) to their ATC. So in the long run equilibrium for a monopolistically competitive firm price is equal to ATC. This means in its long run equilibrium a monopolistically competitive firm similarly to a perfectly competitive firm will make only a normal profit ($0 economic profits).

NOTES

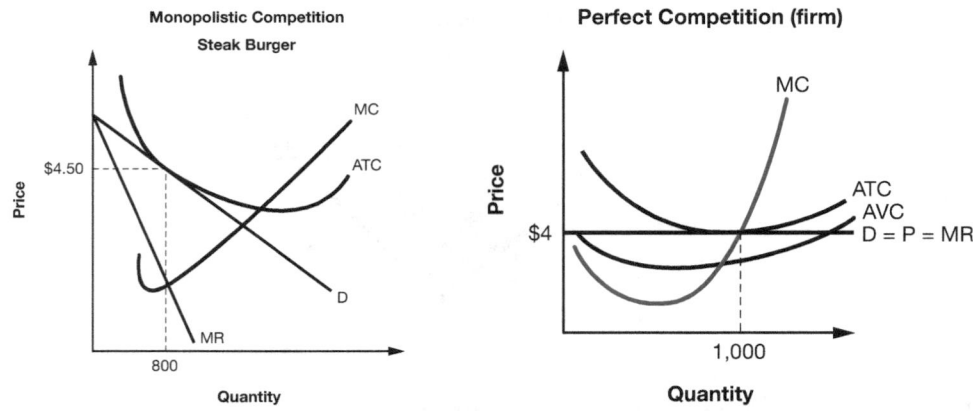

FIGURE 9.3

Efficiency of Monopolistic Competition versus Perfect Competition

Refer to the graph above. Notice that in their long equilibrium both perfect competition and monopolistic competition earn only a normal profit. This is because their demand is tangent (touching at one point) to the ATC. However, since perfect competition has a perfectly elastic demand curve their long run equilibrium is at the bottom of their ATC. So in their long run equilibrium a perfectly competitive firm will produce more and sell at a lower price than a monopolistically competitive firm. In this case you could say that perfect competition is more efficient than monopolistic competition because, in the long run, perfect competition will produce more for less. However, in a perfectly competitive industry all firms produce a homogeneous produce. So whatever burger place you go to you get exactly the same burger. One could argue that in a way monopolistic competition is more efficient than perfect competition because in a monopolistically competitive industry the firms produce a slightly different product. It's nice to try something different once in awhile. As they say "variety is the spice of life."

Assumptions of Oligopoly

1. A few firms dominate the market
2. Product can be homogeneous (standardized) or differentiated
3. Barriers to entry
4. Possible long run economic profits
5. Strategic pricing
6. Interdependent decision making

An oligopoly is in some ways similar to a monopoly and in some ways similar to perfect competition. Oligopolies are closer to a monopoly than perfect competition. However, oligopolies have some characteristics that are unique to oligopolies. Only oligopolies have strategic pricing and interdependent decision making. When an oligopoly is making its pricing decisions it will take the reactions of other firms in the market into consideration. Only an oligopoly will do this. For both perfect competition and monopolistic competition there are too many firms to keep track of. A monopoly does not have to worry about the reaction of other firms because there are no other firms. A good example of an oligopoly producing a homogeneous (standardized) product would be milk. There are only a few firms in the market. One company's milk is almost identical to another company's milk. And significant barriers to entry allow the possibility of long run economic profits. The main barrier to entry for milk and most oligopolies is the start-up cost. The milk companies have vast economies of scale. All of their automated production that lowers the cost per unit is very expensive. That high start-up cost necessary to be competitive with existing firms limits the number of new entrants. An example of an oligopoly that produces a differentiated product would be cars. A few firms dominate the market. They produce a differentiated product. A Ford is different from a Toyota. They are both cars but they have different features and styling. The main difference is the start-up cost. The car companies have vast economies of scale. The robotic arms that do much of the work and lower the cost of a car are expensive. This will make it difficult for someone to start a new car company that could be competitive with existing firms.

Measuring monopoly power:

The Lerner Index

$$\frac{(\text{price} - \text{mc})}{\text{Price}}$$

If both price and MC are equal to $4

Then:

$$\frac{(\$4 - \$4)}{\$4} = 0$$

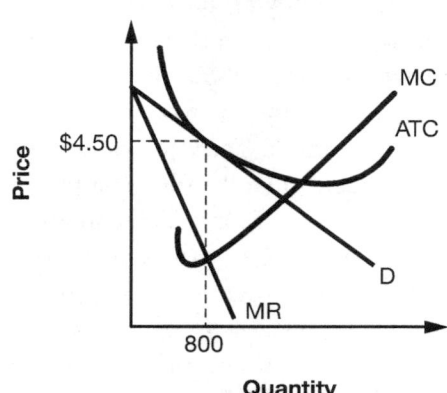

Monopolistic Competition

Steak Burger

FIGURE 9.4

Refer to the graph above. Only a perfectly competitive firm will produce where price equals MC. All firms maximize profit by producing where MR = MC. Only perfect competition has the MR curve as also the price line. Thus, for a perfectly competitive firm producing where MR = MC is also where P = MC. So if you get a 0 for the Lerner Index, you know you have perfect competition. The further away from 0 the more monopoly or pricing power the firm will have.

Concentration Ratios

$$\sum_{i=1}^{4} s_i = s_1 + s_2 + s_3 + s_4$$

Where:

S_1 = the market share of the largest firm

S_2 = the market share of the second largest firm

S_3 = the market share of the third largest firm

S_4 = the market share of the fourth largest firm

Refer to the graph above. To calculate a four firm concentration ratio, just add the market shares of the four largest firms in the market. The larger the number the more market power or control of price firms have. The highest number you could get is 100. If you get a concentration ratio of 100, that means that four firms control the entire market. Concentration ratios are not as accurate as the Herfindahl-Hershman Index; however, they are more often used.

Industry

A = 50 + 50 + 0 + 0 = 100

B = 80 + 20 + 0 + 0 = 100

C = 25 + 25 + 25 + 25 = 100

D = 40 + 20 + 20 + 20 = 100

Refer to the industries above. Industry A is a duopoly. Two firms control the entire market. For industry A the market share is evenly split between the two largest firms. Industry B is also a duopoly; however, one firm is four times larger than the other firm. Industry C has four firms, each have 25 percent of the market. In industry D four firms control the entire market; however, one firm is twice as large as the others. Industries A, B, C, and D all have a four firm concentration ratio of 100. This would indicate that all the industries have the same amount of market power. However, in industry B one firm controls 80 percent of the market. It is almost a monopoly. Clearly industry B would have more control over price than industry C where the firms are everly split in terms of market share. Cases like the above example are rare. But it shows an inaccuracy with concentration ratios.

Herfindahl-Hershman Index

$$\sum_{i=1}^{4} s_i = s_1 + s_2 + s_3 + s_4$$

Where:

S_1^2 = the market share of the largest firm squared

S_2^2 = the market share of the second largest firm squared

S_3^2 = the market share of the third largest firm squared

S_4^2 = the market share of the fourth largest firm squared

Refer to the formula above. To calculate a four firm Herfindahl-Hershman Index just add the market shares squared of the four largest firms in the market. Remember the order of operations. You square first then add! By squaring the market shares you weight the larger market shares more. The highest number you could get is 10,000. If you get a Herfindahl-Hershman Index of 10,000 that means that one firm controls the entire market. The closer you get to 10,000 the closer you get to a monopoly and the more market power exists in the industry.

Industry

$A = 50^2 + 50^2 + 0^2 + 0^2 = 5,000$

$B = 80^2 + 20^2 + 0^2 + 0^2 = 6,800$

$C = 25^2 + 25^2 + 25^2 + 25^2 = 2,500$

$D = 40^2 + 20^2 + 20^2 + 20^2 = 2,800$

Refer to the industries above. Notice that industry B has the highest number indicating that industry B has the most market power and industry C has the lowest number indicating that industry C has the least market power. This is one of the things that our government considers when deciding whether or not to allow companies to merge. They also consider the possibility of improved efficiency of a merger through economies of scale.

Game theory and kinked demand are unique to oligopoly. Both game theory and kinked demand illustrate the concepts of strategic pricing and interdependent decision making which are unique to oligopoly. Remember the ultimate goal of an oligopoly would be to become a monopoly. So oligopolies want to increase their market share or at least maintain their market share.

Game Theory

Jan

	Increase Price	Don't Increase Price
Increase Price	Jan's Profit = $1,000,000 Bill's Profit = $1,000,000	Jan's Profit = $2,000,000 Bill's Profit = $0
Don't Increase Price	Jan's Profit = $0 Bill's Profit = $2,000,000	Jan's Profit = $2,000,000 Bill's Profit = $2,000,000

(Bill — row labels)

Refer to the payoff matrix above. This is a special case of oligopoly known as a duopoly. There are two firms in the market: Jan and Bill. Each firm will take the reaction of their competitor into consideration when making their pricing decisions. The goal of each firm is to maintain or increase their market share. Each firm's dominant strategy will be one that will allow them to maintain or increase their market share. When following their dominant strategy each firm will want to do at least as well or better than their competitor.

Jan

	Increase Price	Don't Increase Price
Increase Price	Jan's Profit = $1,000,000 Bill's Profit = $1,000,000	Jan's Profit = $2,000,000 Bill's Profit = $0
Don't Increase Price	Jan's Profit = $0 Bill's Profit = $2,000,000	Jan's Profit = $2,000,000 Bill's Profit = $2,000,000

(Bill — row labels)

Refer to the payoff matrix above. Jan's choices are the columns. Jan can choose to increase or don't increase her price. Jan's goal is to maintain or increase her market share. Jan's dominant strategy will be one in which no matter how Bill responds Jan will do at least as well as Bill or better.

Jan

	Increase Price	Don't Increase Price
Increase Price	Jan's Profit = $1,000,000 Bill's Profit = $1,000,000	Jan's Profit = $2,000,000 Bill's Profit = $0
Don't Increase Price	Jan's Profit = $0 Bill's Profit = $2,000,000	Jan's Profit = $2,000,000 Bill's Profit = $2,000,000

(Bill — row labels)

Refer to the payoff matrix on the previous page. Bill's choices are the rows. Bill can choose to increase price or don't increase price. Bill's goal is to maintain or increase his market share. Bill's dominant strategy will be one in which no matter how Jan responds Bill will do at least as well as Jan or better.

Jan

		Increase Price	Don't Increase Price
Bill	Increase Price	Jan's Profit = $1,000,000 Bill's Profit = $1,000,000 (1)	Jan's Profit = $2,000,000 Bill's Profit = $0 (2)
	Don't Increase Price	Jan's Profit = $0 Bill's Profit = $2,000,000 (3)	Jan's Profit = $200,000 Bill's Profit = $200,000 (4)

Refer to the payoff matrix above. If Jan decides to increase her price and Bill also increases his price each firm will make $1,000,000 (box 1). This possibility is okay with Jan. However, If Jan decides to increase her price and Bill responds by not increasing his price, all the customers go to Bill. Jan makes $0 and Bill makes $2,000,000 (box 3). Bill becomes a monopoly and Jan loses her business. This possibility is not okay with Jan. She wants to maintain or increase her market share. Jan's other option is to "don't increase price." If Jan does not increase her price but Bill increases his price all the customers will go to Jan. Bill will make $0 and Jan will make $2,000,000 (box 2). Jan becomes a monopoly and Bill gets pushed out of the market. Jan would be very happy with this possibility. If Jan decides to "don't increase price" and Bill also doesn't increase his price, both firms will make $200,000 (box 4). This possibility is okay with Jan. If Jan decides to "don't increase price" no matter how Bill responds Jan will do at least as well or better than Bill. Jan's dominant strategy will be to "don't increase price."

Jan

		Increase Price	Don't Increase Price
Bill	Increase Price	Jan's Profit = $1,000,000 Bill's Profit = $1,000,000 (1)	Jan's Profit = $2,000,000 Bill's Profit = $0 (2)
	Don't Increase Price	Jan's Profit = $0 Bill's Profit = $2,000,000 (3)	Jan's Profit = $200,000 Bill's Profit = $200,000 (4)

Refer to the payoff matrix above. If Bill decides to increase his price and Jan also increases her price each firm will make $1,000,000 (box 1). This possibility is okay with Bill. However, if Bill decides to increase his price and Jan responds by not increasing her price, all the customers go to Jan. Bill makes $0 and Jan makes $2,000,000 (box 2). Jan becomes a monopoly and Bill loses his business. This possibility is not okay with Bill. He wants to maintain or increase his market share. Bill's other option is to "don't increase price." If Bill does not increase his price but Jan increases her price all the customers will go to Bill. Jan will make $0 and Bill will make $2,000,000 (box 3). Bill becomes a monopoly and Jan gets pushed out of the market. Bill would be delighted with this possibility. If Bill decides to "don't increase price" and Jan also doesn't increase her price, both firms will make $200,000 (box 4). This possibility is okay with Bill. If Bill decides to "don't increase price" no matter how Jan responds Bill will do at least as well or better than Jan. Bill's dominant strategy will be to "don't increase price."

Jan

	Increase Price	Don't Increase Price
Increase Price	Jan's Profit = $1,000,000 Bill's Profit = $1,000,000 (1)	Jan's Profit = $2,000,000 Bill's Profit = $0 (2)
Don't Increase Price	Jan's Profit = $0 Bill's Profit = $2,000,000 (3)	Jan's Profit = $200,000 Bill's Profit = $200,000 (4)

Bill (vertical label on left)

Refer to the payoff matrix above. Nash equilibrium is where you end up when both firms follow their dominant strategy. If both Bill and Jan follow their dominant strategy, in Nash equilibrium they will each make $200,000 (box 4). However, if they could agree to both increase their price each firm would make $1,000,000 (box 1). The problem is it is illegal to form a legally binding agreement to have both firms raise price. They could just shake hands and agree to both raise price. The problem is there is a strong incentive to cheat. If Bill cheats, he becomes a monopoly. If Jan cheats, she becomes a monopoly. Therefore, it is unlikely either Jan or Bill will trust the other enough to agree to raise price. So notice even with only two firms in the market, you don't necessarily get higher prices.

Kinked Demand

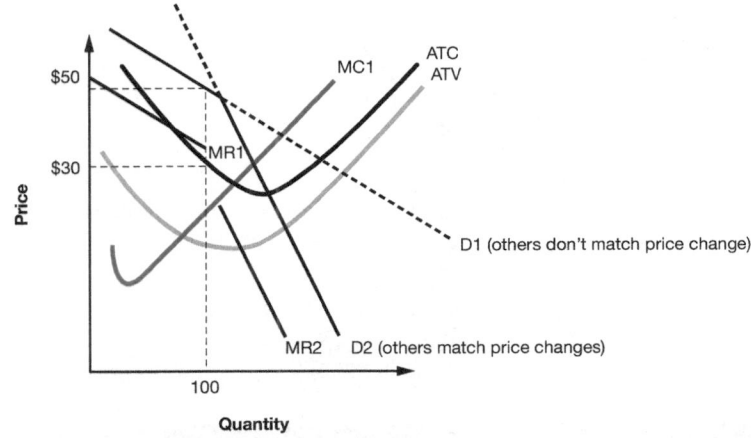

FIGURE 9.5

Refer to the graph above. Kinked demand is unique to oligopoly. Kinked demand illustrates the characteristics of strategic pricing and interdependent decision making which are unique oligopoly. For kinked demand there are two demand curves.

Demand curve one (D1) is relatively elastic. D1 is based on the assumption that others in the market don't match your price changes. So if you lower your price and no one else lowers their price, you will be able to sell a lot more. Demand curve two (D2) is relatively inelastic. D2 is based on the assumption that others in the market will match your price changes. So if you lower your price and everyone else also lowers their price, you will not be able to sell a lot more. The relevant portion of D1 is the upper part. Remember, the goal of oligopoly is to maintain or increase market share. So if you want to increase your price and, therefore, price yourself out of the market your competitors will be happy to let you do that. The relevant portion of D2 is the lower part. Remember, the goal of oligopoly is to maintain or increase their share of the market. So, if you decide to lower your price in order to price your competitors out of the market, they will fight you by lowering their prices as well. The average total cost (ATC) and average variable cost (AVC) curves are U-shaped like any other industry. However, since there are really two demand curves, there will also be two marginal revenue curves. Marginal revenue curve one (MR1) will be parallel to demand curve one (D1). Marginal revenue curve 2 (MR2) will be parallel to demand curve two (D2). Notice there is a gap between MR1 and MR2. Marginal cost one (MC1) will go through the gap. How much will this firm produce? Remember the goal of any business is to maximize profits and all firms maximize profit by producing where MR = MC.

Profit = (P − ATC)Q

Profit = (50 − 30)100

Profit = (20)(100)

Profit = $2,000

Kinked Demand

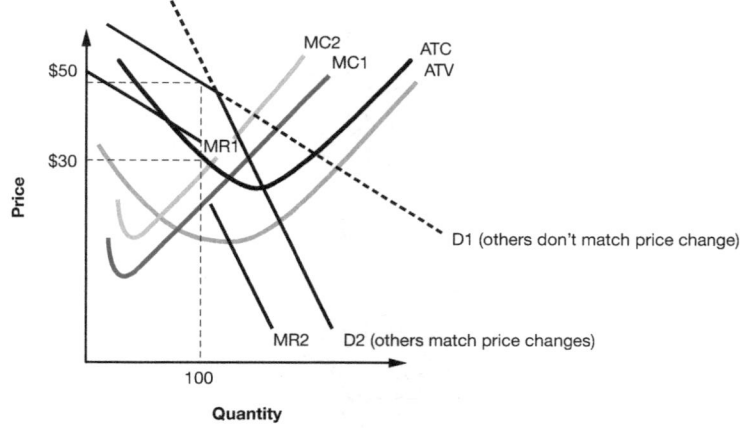

FIGURE 9.6

Refer to the graph above. Suppose that marginal cost shifts up but still within the gap. The firm will produce where MR = MC. So the firm will still produce 100. The firm will still go straight up from the quantity where MR = MC to the demand curve to find price. So the firm will still charge a price of $50 even though their marginal cost has increased. The firm will absorb the cost. This firm will accept a lower profit in the short run in order to stay in the market in hopes of making more mcney in the long run. Remember oligopolies want to maintain or increase their market share. So even if there are only a few firms in the market the oligopoly will not always raise their price.